# KEEP IT POSITIVE

A NEW APPROACH TO SUCCESSFUL PARENTING

Juda Carter, M.A., Esther Chun, J.D.,
and
Rev. Craig Brown, M.Div.

Produced with the support of Shepherd of the Hills Church, 26001 Muirlands Blvd., Mission Viejo, California 92691

*To Carrie, Elizabeth, and William,*
*my treasures and my best teachers.*
*— Juda*

. . .

*To families everywhere, and to Joseph and Ellie, my loves,*
*from whom I have learned so much.*
*— Esther*

. . .

*To God, the perfect parent of us all.*
*— Craig*

# TABLE OF CONTENTS

# ACKNOWLEDGEMENTS

## From Juda Carter

As with so many projects of this nature, the people who helped and nurtured me along the way were invaluable to this book. I first want to thank the students I met in my career who helped me learn about positive behavior support. These include Tim, Sarah, Derek, Alex, John, Ryan, and Emily. Without them, this would never have been possible. I also do not want to fail to mention Dr. LeeAnn Christian. As a professional in Positive Behavior Management, she was an example of someone who believed in children's desire to learn and behave and nurtured that belief in others.

I also want to give my heartfelt thanks to my co-authors, Reverend Craig Brown and Esther Chun. Craig worked on and supported this project from its simple beginnings and always encouraged me. Esther Chun and her family have been an amazing source of love and support. Esther's work ethic and dedication were always an inspiration to me. Julie Major, a parent facilitator in our classes, contributed ideas, work, and love to this book. Many thanks to Julie and her family for the time and effort involved.

I also want to thank a host of parents who believed in *Keep It Positive* during the years of writing and revising. These include Alicia and Jim Riding, Dave and Julie Mazza, David and Megan Carter, Julie and Tom Major, Ronee Baum, Juliette Widholm, Carrie Havens, and many others. Finally, I want to thank Tom Boatman for his invaluable reading and responding to our drafts. Most importantly I want to thank my husband, Reverend Jerry Carter, for everything he is and has been to me and our family. Your unfailing love and support have guided me in this and many paths in our lives.

## From Esther Chun

More than anything else, this book has been a labor of love for me and for my family. We are so grateful to have learned this method and to have experienced so many of its benefits that we wanted to share it with others. My husband and I thank God every day for how things have changed in our household.

I am indebted, of course, to Juda Carter and Rev. Craig Brown, for making the method available by teaching the class. I thank Juda for continuing to inspire and teach me with her caring and energetic ways, and for the opportunity to participate in the writing of this book. In addition to those already mentioned by Juda, I also want to thank Eric Wolff, whose edits and opinions were invaluable to improving our work. Thank you also to my friends and family, for their belief in and support of our project. Love and gratitude to my husband and best friend, David, whose help with the children enabled me to spend the many hours it took to write, revise, and edit, and whose support and love, along with my children, are the great treasures of my life. Finally, love and thanks to my wonderful, loving children, who are ultimately my inspiration for this book.

## From Rev. Craig Brown

Having an idea spring to life in written word must be one of the heights of God's creative gifts! We are a creative people, blessed in the image of God. What a joy it has been to share this journey with two of the most creative freethinkers I know in Esther Chun and Juda Carter. Their commitment to this project from the beginning has been remarkable to witness and confirms to me once again the creative capacity that humans are endowed with by their God. Esther's attention to detail and her ability to hear words for the first time, even though she has heard them a hundred times before, does not cease to amaze me. Juda's excitement about raising children with a positive approach is infectious. She truly is an evangelist for raising children in a manner consistent with God's care and love for us.

I cannot even imagine putting pen to paper without acknowledging my own family, which has tolerated my own failures as a parent in so many ways. Both my son, David, and my daughter, Rachel, will have jewels in their crowns for the long-suffering they endured until I learned how to be a better and more effective parent. Being the child of a pastor is enough of a burden! Of course, many thanks to my partner and the love of my life, Bettina, for sharing this journey of parenthood! Her willingness to be a part of this crazy life of ministry has always been a comfort and a blessing to me each day.

# ABOUT THE AUTHORS

This study guide came out of the experience of the authors. Juda Carter, M.A., Psychology — Marriage, Family, and Child Counseling, has been a Special Education consultant to schools and parents since the early 1990's. She is also a lecturer at California State University-Fullerton in the Department of Special Education. Mrs. Carter has taught positive behavior support and has implemented the principles in schools as an administrator and as a consultant. She has extensive experience working with students with significant behavioral issues. Mrs. Carter often thought that research-based behavioral support would benefit all parents. She decided to apply the principles and techniques to parenting her own three children and saw amazing benefits for her family. Believing that the principles of positive behavior support were reinforced in Christianity and the lessons of the Bible, she shared some of the ideas with her pastor, the Reverend Craig Brown.

Reverend Brown is the senior pastor at Shepherd of the Hills United Methodist Church in Mission Viejo, California. Rev. Brown asked Mrs. Carter to conduct a parenting class at his church, and they decided to teach the principles of positive behavior support together. The response from the class was phenomenal. The parents who participated continue to meet monthly to support one another in applying the principles of positive behavior support.

Esther Chun, a former attorney, credentialed elementary schoolteacher, and parent, participated in the first class taught by Mrs. Carter and Rev. Brown. After successfully applying the parenting principles to her own two children, she developed a passion to share what she has learned with other parents.

If you are reading this for the first time, our hope is that you will learn to encourage your children to behave appropriately, to forgive them when they make mistakes, and to create a home environment that is filled with love—the same kind of love that God offers us freely. We have worked tirelessly to prepare this information to help you achieve these goals. We welcome your feedback, as we know we all learn from one another.

# HOW TO USE THIS BOOK

*Keep It Positive* is a parenting manual that presents a new approach to parenting that is best utilized in a holistic fashion. Each chapter adds information and builds skills from the previous chapter and is important to the methodology. We encourage you to read the entire book to understand how to implement the philosophy. When reading books on parenting, many parents may be tempted to skip to the portion of the book that focuses on a specific problem that they are experiencing. We ask you to resist this temptation and read this book chronologically.

It is important to read *Keep It Positive* chronologically because it presents a methodology of behavior change that is most powerful when practiced in its entirety. Understanding why your children behave the way they do, and understanding how your actions can either encourage or diminish that behavior is the key to implementing the positive behavior change you want to achieve. All the chapters of this book deal with significant elements that fit together to create one powerful methodology.

In this book, we address specific issues like sibling rivalry, getting out the door, chores, untruthfulness, homework, etc. However, these examples are not meant to stand as an exhaustive list of all the possible ways to deal with these issues. Instead, *Keep It Positive* gives you a framework with many tools to use, often using various situations to illustrate the methodology. Because of this, you will want to give careful consideration to all the examples in the book, even though you may not be experiencing problems with such behaviors at present. Each of the examples is important because each illustrates different facets of the methodology. Once you have a strong understanding of the methodology, you will be able to apply it to any situation.

Parents who have been the most successful with this method have solidly understood and practiced all the elements in this book in harmony. As will be discussed throughout the book, the more you practice the skills presented here, the easier they become, and the more benefits your whole family will experience. We encourage you to try the skills and practice, practice, practice. In this way, you will experience the rich reward of a positive and peaceful household.

# INTRODUCTION

## *A New Approach To Successful Parenting*

In this guide, we will help you change the way you see your child and her behavior, and your role and actions as a parent. This new vision will enable you to change the ineffective and possibly destructive habits that may have entered your home. It will help you create an environment in which your child will be encouraged and inspired, rather than coerced or forced, to mature. In this way, you will allow your child to truly internalize the values you seek to instill.

Many parents come to our classes having tried time-outs, counting to three, consequences and punishments, and found that nothing really works for every situation. Many of them are exhausted and frustrated, feeling that their vision of being an effective and loving parent is not being realized as they had imagined. After consistently implementing the *Keep It Positive* method, however, parents feel a sense of empowerment because now they understand how to encourage appropriate behavior and what they must do differently to support their children.

Positive behavior support is the key to understanding how to effectively manage your children's behavior at every age, create peace in your home, and preserve loving, caring relationships with your children that will follow them into adulthood. It is a method that works for every behavioral issue that occurs with children of every age, because it provides a flexible structure based on scientifically researched principles of human behavior. S.W. Bijou writes in *The International Encyclopedia of Education*, "Research has shown that the **most effective way** to reduce problem behavior in children is to **strengthen desirable behavior through positive reinforcement**, rather than trying to weaken undesirable behavior using aversive or negative processes." This is not a permissive system. We ask you to set high expectations and to encourage your children to achieve them. It is an effective, proactive, and respectful form of discipline.

It is also a method of parenting based on love and one that is reflected in Christianity. We generally do not find God to be an entity who establishes boundaries and then strikes down all who fail to meet His expectations. It is clear from even a cursory reading of the Scriptures that God faithfully communicates expectations and then does everything possible, barring the use of force, to help people fulfill those expectations. None of us would describe God as "permissive." He is open, honest, faithful, and hopeful that all of His children will live up to their greatest potential for the redeeming of the world. God has been a positive parent from the beginning, but no one would describe Him as "weak," "passive," or "absent." God is the original parent, and the best the world has ever known.

No behavioral method can create perfect children, and you should be wary of any method that promises to do so. The strength of this method, however, is that it promotes **long-term** internal growth and lasting success. Your child will grow with an internal sense of responsibility, a respect for you and others, and a healthy patience for his own short-comings. Most importantly, he will mature with the strength that comes from knowing that he is unconditionally loved. When you have successfully employed these methods, you will end each day at peace with the quality of the job you have done, secure in the knowledge that you are building the foundations of a strong, loving relationship that will last a lifetime.

This method requires an investment of effort and a willingness to see things differently. As you work through this process, remember that with any new skill you learn, it takes plenty of practice to do well. This is not a quick fix. It is a new way of thinking and interacting with your child. It is about becoming a loving, positive force in your family. Each section in this book is devoted to learning another aspect of these skills to practice and implement. We invite you to join with your spouse, your friends, and family members to support one another in the goal of positive parenting.

*Chapter One*

WHY BE POSITIVE?

*Positive vs. Negative Models of Reinforcement*

*Point your kids in the right direction—
when they're old they won't be lost.*

—The Message, *inspired by Proverbs 22:6*

Why Be Positive When You Interact with Your Children?

- It is proven to be the most effective way to change behavior.
- It will internalize strong values.
- It strengthens your relationship with your child.
- It is well supported in theology.

The *Keep It Positive* method of parenting involves a new way of thinking and a new way of disciplining your children. Before we delve into the principles of the method, it is helpful to review the typical ways parents discipline children in our culture today.

## Typical Discipline Techniques

The two most common methods of discipline used in American culture are "Cost Response" and "Progressive Discipline." These methods are widely practiced today, although there is no research to support their efficacy. Let us examine how they work.

In the Cost Response method, a negative consequence, the "cost," is given for a negative behavior. This method is commonly used in most public schools, and particularly in elementary schools. The method may take on many forms, from "pulling cards" (where teachers take one of four colored cards each time a child engages in unwanted behavior), to separation from others, to losing a privilege. Parents often employ the Cost Response method by giving "time-outs," taking away privileges, or verbally reprimanding children as punishments for inappropriate behavior.

**Diagram A:**

# Cost Response

Inappropriate Behavior ⟶ Punishment (Cost)

*Message child receives is that she is "bad," deserves to be punished, or that the teacher/parent is "mean or unfair." Focus on better behavior is blurred.*

Progressive Discipline is also a common methodology for behavior intervention in American culture. It involves a tiered level of punishments to fit the severity of the negative behavior. The greater the infraction, the greater the punishment. It is implemented regularly in most schools at the secondary level. For example, for tardiness, a student receives detention. For truancy, he receives a suspension. For drug possession, he may be expelled. This method is also apparent in most criminal justice systems. The greater the crime, the greater the punishment. Although we are not advocating eliminating punishment for crimes, we do believe that punishment generally fails to change behavior. Recidivism rates in United States prisons are a strong indication that punishment, while it may serve other purposes, does not change behavior.[1] Naturally, given a better alternative, most parents would not choose to run their homes like a prison.

In the home, Progressive Discipline is usually handled more impulsively and with anger. "Stop hitting your sister! Go to your room!" or "I can't believe you talked to me that way. You're grounded for a month!" Or sometimes it's given with less anger and more method. For example, for not cleaning up, a child loses her toy; for not brushing her teeth, she gets a time-out; for hitting, she gets a spanking.

**Diagram B:**

# Progressive Discipline

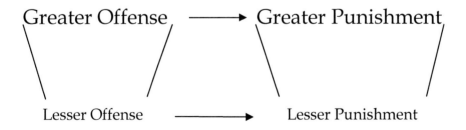

Greater Offense ⟶ Greater Punishment

Lesser Offense ⟶ Lesser Punishment

## Advantages and Disadvantages
## of Traditional Punitive Models

The Cost Response and Progressive Discipline methods of behavior management are highly attractive to many busy parents because they seem to work immediately. When a parent yells at a child or punishes her with a time-out or other means, it usually gets the child's attention and makes her perform the desired behavior. Many parents are drawn to this method because it seems to work, but it works only temporarily and at a cost. The child only complies because she is afraid of her parents' anger.

Problems often emerge later, when instead of learning the value of responsibility or kindness, a child may repeat the negative behavior until she is punished. Sometimes she may even intentionally perform the very behavior that the parent is trying to eradicate, despite the consequences. The parent is now faced with power struggles or passive-aggressive behavior[2] and is then compelled to increase the consequences to keep the method effective. More often, these methods stop working altogether, sometimes sooner rather than later.

Not only are these methods ineffective in the long run or difficult to implement, but as shown in Table 1, the disadvantages of these methods can be detrimental to a child's development. Matters often come to a head when a child becomes a teenager and does not have the strong, loving relationship with her parents that would have helped keep her feeling supported and out of trouble. Parents may then find that time-outs, threats, and consequences do not work, and that rebellion, shared anger, or secrecy may rule the day. To the surprise of many parents, children who may have once seemed compliant and obedient may suddenly act up in school, or become angry, unmotivated, or depressed. While no system is fail-safe, studies show that the better the **relationship** parents have with their children, the less at risk a child will be during the turbulent years of adolescence.[3] Instead of bringing parents closer to their children, however, negative methods generally create division and distance.

### Table 1
### Pros and Cons of Traditional Punitive Models [4]

| Advantages | Disadvantages |
|---|---|
| 1. Seems to work short term on the particular task or behavior. Immediate results. | 1. Does not usually work long term. Consequences often need to be increased to stay effective. |
| 2. Easy to implement at start, with little practice and training on parent's part. | 2. Often requires continued warning, threatening, and punishing. |
| | 3. Teaches children that they may do what they can get away with until there is a consequence. |
| | 4. Can create feelings of inadequacy or an unhealthy desire to be perfect. |

|  | 5. Can create judgmental attitudes toward others.<br><br>6. Promotes rebellion, power struggles, and passive-aggressive behavior.<br><br>7. Can create negative feelings toward the task, behavior, or value that the parent is trying to teach.<br><br>8. Can create negative feelings toward parent. Child often **believes** he is unloved.<br><br>9. Not generalizable. Does not create the generally desired value in the child. Only tends to work for the specific task or behavior.<br><br>10. Models negative problem-solving behavior. Teaches children that the way to deal with problems is to punish the source of the problem.<br><br>11. Sets children up for failure because punitive methods are reactive and anticipate noncompliance. |
| --- | --- |

In contrast, the advantages of positive behavior support far outweigh the disadvantages as seen in Table 2.

**Table 2**
**Pros and Cons of Positive Behavior Support**

| Advantages | Disadvantages |
|---|---|
| 1. Works long term. | 1. Implementation takes time and commitment on the parent's part. Takes patience to change parenting practices and perspectives. |
| 2. No artificial consequences required because children internalize the desired value; they behave well because they want to, not because they have to. | 2. Results take time. May not see instant results. It will take time for children's behavior to level out. |
| 3. No need to tell children to do something many times before they do it. | 3. Requires parental analysis and reflection. |
| 4. Empowers children and encourages them to be independent. | |
| 5. Encourages positive feelings toward the desired task, behavior, or value. | |
| 6. Encourages a healthy patience with own shortcomings and a habit of working on them. Does not lead to unhealthy perfectionism. | |

7. Helps develop patience for and understanding of others' shortcomings. Children do not feel the need to judge.

8. Creates positive feelings toward parent. Children feel unconditionally loved.

9. Generalizable. For example, children will not only dress themselves, but may also do their homework because they have learned the general values of being responsible and independent.

10. Models control of emotions and problem solving for children.

11. Prepares children for success because the method proactively focuses on appropriate behavior.

Understandably, many parents use punitive methods because they believe punitive discipline works. Yet, many of those same parents remain "fed up" with their children because they feel they constantly need to fight in order to get them to behave well. "I'm so frustrated! It seems like the only thing that works is to yell at them or take things away! I hate being like this, but I feel like I have no other choice." This is a sentiment expressed by many parents during the first sessions of our classes. There is a better way.

That better way is evident in the life and ministry of Jesus Christ, who gave us a distinctly different and positive message. The negative techniques discussed previously fail to mirror the Christian ethic. Many common parenting processes only respond to children when they fail to meet certain expectations. These are often the only times they receive any feedback on their behavior. In contrast, Jesus told His followers, "Let your light shine before men in such a way that they may see your **good works**, and glorify your Father who is in heaven" (Matthew 5:16). Instead of modeling our life around the avoidance of mistakes (Cost Response or Progressive Discipline), Jesus invites us to imitate His life and, in turn, to live a life worthy of imitation. We want to live a life that becomes a beacon of what *to do*, rather than what not to do. We want to focus our parenting energy on helping our children do what is right rather than simply telling them what not to do wrong.

Jesus' actions are a testament to His focus on the positive. Instead of condemning Zacchaeus as a corrupt, greedy tax collector, He gave him the ultimate honor of dining at his home and encouraged him to do the right thing (Luke 19:1-10). Instead of punishing a prostitute, Jesus accepted her hospitality by allowing her to wash His feet with perfume, and affirmed her good act at the protest of His disciples

(Luke 7:36-50). Jesus even rescued an adulterous woman from the "lawful" punishment of stoning, declaring, "If any one of you is without sin, let him be the first to throw a stone at her," and telling her to "Go now and leave your life of sin" (John 8:3-11). Jesus knew the tremendous power of positive reinforcement and teaching to truly change the lives and behavior of real people.

*One Parent's Experience with Positive Parenting:*

*"I remember being exposed to different positive parenting methods years ago and thinking, 'This will never work with my son! No one understands how intense and difficult he is. He's way more intense and demanding than other kids, and consequences are the only things that work for him.'" After a few years of clear expectations, negative consequences, and time-outs, however, her five-year-old child suddenly burst out, "I wish I had never been born! You don't love me because I'm a terrible, terrible boy! I think that I should run out into the street and get hit by a car so I won't be trouble to anyone!" Obviously, this mom was devastated and was ready for a change.*

*After implementing the Keep It Positive methodology, life in her household completely changed. "I am so grateful to this program because my son never says he feels unloved anymore. Both my children now understand that they are unconditionally loved. They now want to be responsible, not because they are afraid of me, but because they know what we expect and what it means to be responsible. They want to behave well, they love to hear our positive affirmation, and they actually behave better than they ever have before. Instead of anger, lecturing, time-outs, passive-aggressive behavior, and temper tantrums, we now have peace, trust, respect, and love for each other. My kids are taking responsibility, often of their own initiative. They are not perfect, they are a work in progress – like I am – but the positive experiences now vastly outnumber the negative ones. They know that I am always on their side, and I will teach and help them to grow instead of punishing them for not growing fast enough. Besides this, we're just having a lot more fun and I'm really enjoying my kids again!"*

## What Positive Behavior Support Means

Positive behavior support with the *Keep It Positive* program is not a magic trick. It is a total mind shift that reaps genuine, long-term results. *Keep It Positive* is a way of changing yourself so that you begin to **understand** your children's behavior, rather than simply **reacting** to it. When you understand that a child's behavior always has a purpose, you can deal with the causes of the behavior rather than just the symptoms. When you understand why children behave the way they do, you can learn how to create an environment that encourages appropriate behavior and discourages inappropriate behavior.

In the *Keep It Positive* program, you will learn a specific method and structure to employ when analyzing and dealing with your children's behavior. You will learn how to:

- Use the basic principles of human behavior to inform your parenting and understand why your children behave the way they do.
- Analyze your child's behavior and discover the root issues behind it.
- Teach and model your clear expectations.
- Set clear boundaries.
- Encourage positive behavior with specific positive verbal reinforcement.
- Structure your routines to encourage positive behavior.
- Use natural and logical consequences in an effective way.
- Foster a relationship where true communication takes place.

*Keep It Positive* is a proactive, rather than a reactive, method of parenting. While many methods punish children for their negative behavior, the *Keep It Positive* method helps children find success in positive behavior. As a result, your children will be able to internalize the values and behaviors you want them to learn, instead of being dependent on external forces of shame, disappointment, or fear to motivate good behavior. Your children will learn to be responsible, loving, caring individuals, not because they fear consequences, but because they truly value those characteristics and feel good about themselves when they practice them.

## Exercise I

Begin by analyzing the behaviors that are causing you the most difficulty. Then take note of how you presently respond to those behaviors. The steps below are coordinated to help you observe yourself in interactions with your children. Take some time to carefully document your reactions. These are the first steps to making a positive change.

First, write down one behavior that is causing the most difficulty and discord in your home.

_____

_____

_____

Now write your exact response to that behavior (words you used, what you did, etc.).

**Behavior:**

| What your child did or did not do | When it happened | What you did (Be specific) |
|---|---|---|
|  |  |  |

In Chapter Two, you will learn to better understand your children by exploring some basic principles of human behavior and how they should impact your approach to parenting. You will also review the behavioral chart you completed and begin an analysis of that behavior.

### Chapter One Summary

- Positive behavior support is the **most effective** way to change a child's long-term behavior.[5] Although no system can guarantee perfect behavior, this system has been proven to be the most effective means of encouraging appropriate behavior.
- Positive behavior support is not only grounded in the science of human behavior, but also on a foundation of Christian principles and unconditional love.
- Positive behavior support takes practice and patience.
- Negative, reactive methods of parenting can be damaging for children in the long run and have been proven to be **less effective**.
- Positive behavior support helps children internalize the values you want them to learn and builds them up, instead of degrading or demeaning them.
- As shown in Table 2, the advantages of positive behavior support go beyond mere compliance with the particular desired behavior.

..........................................

## Chapter Two

# GIVE POSITIVE ATTENTION TO GOOD BEHAVIOR

## *Principles of Positive Behavior Support*

*"Teacher, which is the great commandment in the Law?" And He said to him, "'You shall love the Lord your God with all your heart, and with all your soul, and with all your mind.' This is the great and foremost commandment. The second is like it, 'You shall love your neighbor as yourself.' On these two commandments depend the whole Law and the Prophets."*

*— Matthew 22:36-40, NASB*

When Jesus was asked what the greatest commandment was, He replied by stating something every Jewish person in His day would know. Loving the Lord your God is the most important commandment. Additionally, He states that loving your neighbor is just as important. Take note that Jesus says that all "the Laws and the Prophets" depend on these two imperatives. In other words, every rule in the Bible can be attributed to these two statements. And each one is stated positively rather than negatively. When God shares His expectations with His children, we find that they are often positive. God explains what **to do** instead of what **not to do**. When it comes to summarizing the moral commands of the scripture, Jesus does so in a positive fashion.

**Give positive attention to positive behavior.**

Give very little or no attention to negative behavior at the time it is occurring, because:

- Positive attention given to positive behavior will increase the behavior.

- Any attention given to inappropriate behavior will increase that behavior.

As we discussed in the first chapter, punishment and negative consequences do not work in the long term and have negative effects on your children and your relationship with them. So what do you do instead? In positive behavior support, we use positive reinforcement to encourage good behavior, eliminating the need to use punishment as a tool. In this chapter, we will focus on the basic principles of positive behavior support, to help you understand why positive reinforcement works.

---

## Principles of Positive Behavior Support

1. All behavior is purposeful.
2. Any behavior that receives either positive or negative attention will increase.
3. Behavior change first begins with the parents, not the children.

---

## 1. All behavior is purposeful.

The most basic principle of positive behavior support is that all behavior is purposeful. Everything we do has a purpose. The purpose may be to communicate something, to get something, to avoid unpleasant outcomes, or to express our feelings. We work to get paid, we give gifts to make others happy, we drive near the speed limit to avoid speeding tickets, we express anger to vent emotions or because we want to change something.

Children's behavior follows the same rule. Everything children do, they do for a purpose. It may be to get our attention, to express an emotion, to get what they want, or to avoid something unpleasant. Children generally do not do things just to make our lives miserable, although it can sometimes feel that way. They do not behave inappropriately because they want to be bad, manipulative, selfish, or mean. They behave inappropriately because they get something from it, because the behavior is the means to an end.

Alex cries when Mom goes to work because he wants to communicate his unhappiness about the separation, and because he gets something out of her response. Jenny plays with her food because she likes the way the food feels in her fingers. Jake throws a tantrum at the store to vent his anger and to change Dad's mind when he refuses to buy him candy. Sara lies about hitting her sister because she wants to avoid punishment. These are logical and effective, albeit self-interested behaviors. Children do not consciously behave inappropriately, rather they use inappropriate behavior to satisfy their needs.

This is consistent with what research tells us about human behavior. Behavior can be described in a simple fashion that is known as the "ABC" of behavior. A is the Antecedent, B is the behavior, and C is the consequence. When Jake throws a tantrum in the store, the A (antecedent) may be a desire to gain something (candy) or to express his frustration. The B (behavior) is the tantrum. The C (consequence) is what you do. If Dad buys Jake the candy, the consequence of Jake's behavior is that he gets what he wants. A consequence that satisfies a child's desire encourages the child to repeat the behavior. This simple formula can be applied to almost any behavior your child displays.

Think about some of your children's most difficult behaviors. What might they be trying to communicate? Are they attempting to gain access to something or escape some unwanted activity? As you review the exercise from Chapter One, you can begin to understand the purposes of the behaviors you have charted. By identifying the purpose of the child's behavior and changing your response, you are already following two of the above principles of the *Keep It Positive* method. Understanding the purposes of your children's actions will help you develop responses that account for the causes, as well as the symptoms of the behavior. This method will also help you see your children's behavior in a neutral light. What your children are doing makes sense because they get something out of it. In Chapter Five, we will revisit this principle to help you understand the often hidden messages in your children's communications.

## 2. Any behavior that is given either positive or negative attention will increase.

In academic studies of human behavior, it is always noted that any behavior we reinforce, either positively or negatively, will increase. What does reinforcing mean? For our purposes, reinforcing simply means giving some sort of attention to your child, either good or bad. This attention can take on many forms: giving a child an object, touching, a verbal reprimand, verbal praise, a time-out, anger, laughter, even a pointed look. As we will explore below, if you give specific, genuinely positive attention to good behavior, the good behavior will increase. Most parents understand this to be true. Surprisingly, however, if you pay **any** kind of attention to negative behavior, that negative behavior will also increase. For negative behavior, **any** attention you give equals reinforcement.

## Positive Behavior Increases with Positive Attention

The most effective way to eliminate negative behavior is to encourage the corresponding positive behavior with positive attention. If your child has a habit of hitting, specifically give attention to and encourage any safe and cooperative play. If he has a habit of jumping on the couch, specifically give attention to using the couch appropriately. If he has a habit of screaming, specifically praise him when he uses an appropriate voice.

Children are hard-wired to seek out positive attention from the minute they are born. When infants smile, they invite us to interact with them. So we smile back, we talk to them, we tell them how cute and wonderful they are. Our positive attention encourages infants to smile again and again. In this way, infants learn an interaction that is so crucial to their development. The positive behavior of the smile increases when we reinforce it positively.

This is also true of all other behaviors. When we immediately, specifically, and genuinely give verbal praise for using an indoor voice, for quickly completing a requested task, for sharing, or for being flexible, these behaviors will increase. "Hey, John! Great job sitting down to do your homework on your own. I like how independent and responsible you're becoming." John feels valued for acting responsibly and will be much more likely to be responsible, not only with his homework, but in other areas as well.

"I know that you really wanted to stay longer at the park, Alice. It's fun to play, isn't it? But I really like the way you came to the car when I said it was time to leave, even though you didn't want to. That shows me that you are being a good listener." Alice feels good about herself for listening even though she might still be angry about leaving. Although she may have whined about leaving, she will be much more willing to leave without protest the next time. When we positively acknowledge **any approximation** to a desired behavior, the desired behavior will increase.

## Negative Behavior Increases with Positive Attention

The way you respond to negative behavior will determine whether your child will continue to act that way. Because baby Jake's cry is the only way he knows how to express his discomfort, Mom uses her skills to discover the problem and address it. Jake then continues to use this necessary crying to communicate, because Mom has reinforced it.

When **three-year-old** Michelle cries, however, Dad would like to teach her the new skill of using her words to communicate. But if Dad gives positive attention to Michelle's crying (giving her what she wants), Michelle will continue to use crying to get what she wants. Her crying may even increase because she has learned that crying is an effective way to communicate and satisfy her needs. A more effective strategy for Michelle's dad would be to ignore the crying and, at a different time, as will be discussed in Chapter Four, teach her to use polite words to make her wishes known.

## Negative Behavior Also Increases
## with Negative Attention

Does negative attention (lecturing, punishing, yelling) work to eliminate unwanted behavior? As parents, we often mistakenly believe it will. A child does something wrong, the child is punished, and the behavior stops. Although this sounds logical, in reality, the opposite is generally true. A behavior that is given **any** attention, even negative attention, actually tends to increase over time. For example, John's mom goes through the daily ritual of reminding, requesting, or demanding that her ten-year-old son complete his homework. Even with this negative attention, every day John continues to procrastinate or passively refuses to complete the work. Fed up, Mom decides to sit with him every night to make sure he gets it done. This one-on-one attention, though presumably positive, is very reinforcing. John would rather have this attention than finish the task by himself. Although John's mom wanted to teach him to be independent and responsible, John is now less so because Mom gives him lots of attention for being dependent and irresponsible. The very behaviors Mom is trying to eliminate (avoidance, procrastination, dependency) are inadvertently being encouraged.

This is consistent with many parents' experiences, which is probably why you are reading this book. How many times have you told your children to throw away their trash, stop jumping on the couch, or stop calling names, and find that the behavior does not change? Or if it does change, how many times do your children go behind your back to do what they want anyway?

Why don't children change their behavior even when we punish them? The major reason is that children crave the attention of their parents more than anything in the world. As their primary providers of sustenance, guidance, and love, parents are the most powerful and important people in the eyes of their children. As Gary Chapman and Ross Campbell note in their book, *The Five Love Languages of Children*, children crave our **unconditional** acceptance so much that they often push the limits to test the strength of our love. The beauty of the *Keep It Positive* method is that loving responses to a child's behavior are built into interactions, and a loving and trusting relationship is therefore established. When children do not receive the positive acceptance they need, they will often use behavior to secure **any** attention from parents, positive or negative.

Punishment also does not change behavior over time because children and parents often fall into patterns of ineffective interaction. A child acts inappropriately, the parent punishes the negative behavior, the child repeats the behavior, the parent repeats the punishment. These patterns of ineffective interactions can become habitual. Parent and child each play a role, and nowhere in the pattern of interaction does the cycle get broken. Nowhere does the parent teach the child the expected behavior and give the child encouragement, attention, and structure to behave appropriately. Consequently, the child gets used to this habitual way of interacting with the parent and repeats it. In the *Keep It Positive* method, you will learn a new way of interacting that will help you break old habits. You will learn to encourage your child to behave well and you will learn to use clear expectations, boundaries, and logical consequences to address inappropriate behavior.

### 3. Behavior change first begins with the parents, not the children.

Children behave the way they do for a purpose. Because that purpose is being fulfilled in some way (often a way not intended by the child or the adult) the child continues or increases the behavior. We cannot force a child to change. All that we truly have control over are our own actions and responses. When we examine our own behavior and the child's environment, we can discover what we are doing to perpetuate undesirable behavior. Behavioral change depends on the parents. This may be the most difficult concept to grasp in positive behavior support.

Your response might be, "I'm reading this to change my child's behavior, not my own. I want him to act appropriately, to obey me, and to do things when I ask him to. It doesn't matter what I do, or what his situation is, he still needs to learn to mind me." Sure, if your children were robots, they would do exactly what you want, when you want it. Luckily, children are much more interesting and more complex than that. Instead of becoming frustrated that your children do not automatically listen, try to understand that they continue to act inappropriately because somehow you have inadvertently made it beneficial for them to act that way.

Understand this concept, and you will begin to see that

the only way to change your child's behavior is to change your own. It begins by positively reinforcing the behavior you want to see, and ignoring the behavior you want to eliminate. The concept is not easy to grasp, especially when you are in the practice of punishing inappropriate behavior. However, when you begin to change your behavior, your child's behavior will change as well.

## A Parent's Most Important Behavior Change
## Positive Verbal Reinforcement

The most important way to change your own behavior in regard to your children is to begin giving them Positive Verbal Reinforcement (PVR). PVR is the most effective way to effect a long-term change in behavior. It's as simple as: noticing any good things that your children do and then 1) specifically, 2) verbally, 3) positively, and 4) genuinely reinforcing it. If your eight-year-old helps your four-year-old with her seat belt, you can say, "I like how you are being a helper to Mary by putting on her seat belt." Here, you are using positive words ("I like") to specifically state what your eight-year-old has done ("being a helper to Mary by putting on her seat belt"). This is much more effective than "Good job," or "Nice work." Linking the specific action to a characteristic you want to encourage (being helpful) gives moral structure to your praise and helps your children internalize the value you want them to learn.

In order to be effective, the PVR needs to be quiet, calm, and genuine. While the younger your child is, the more enthusiastic your praise can be, it is important to let the praise speak for itself as your child matures. At two years, genuine enthusiasm about a new behavior is appropriate. "Wow, Jessica! I like the way you put your clothes in the hamper right away! You listened so well!" As the child matures, a PVR should be calmer, though always genuine. "Andrew, I so appreciate how you help out by putting your clothes in the hamper without being asked. You're really doing a good job being responsible." You want to be calm with older children because an overexcited, excessively demonstrative PVR will often ring false in the ears of older children.

A PVR must also be specific to the behavior you want to encourage. "Good job! You're terrific!" are responses that are non-specific and effusive. They do not tell the child what behavior was appreciated, or what behavior to repeat the next time. Instead, you can say, "I like the way you said please when you asked for more water." This way, the child knows exactly what to do the next time.

Responses like "You're so smart!" can even be detrimental to a child's growth because they focus on what the child is naturally born with (which is completely out of the child's control), instead of on the child's behavior. Research shows that children who are given this kind of general praise can actually underperform because of that praise. These children can be so focused on looking smart that they may have difficulty coping with failure and are sometimes afraid to try new things.[6] In the *Keep It Positive* model, we focus on a child's effort and behavior, which the child can control. "I like the way you worked hard on that math problem even though it was difficult. You stuck to it and it paid off" is an example of a specific PVR that praises the child's effort and behavior. In this way, you can teach your child the persistence, deferred gratification, and resilience that it takes to deal with potential failures.

Not only does the PVR need to be specific, quiet, and calm, but it must also be genuine and devoid of any implied criticism of the child. When Mom says to twelve-year-old Nancy, "I see you stopped eating all that junk food," she is pointing out Nancy's previous negative behavior instead of focusing on the positive changes she has made. Imbedded in her "compliment" is a criticism of Nancy's prior behavior. A true PVR must be 100% positive. So instead, Mom says to Nancy, "I like the way you are playing tennis and eating healthy foods. I bet you are feeling better every day." Mom is now focusing on Nancy's positive behavior and on the good results they inspire. Imagine how much more encouraged Nancy would feel given this response. Table 3 contrasts examples of effective PVR with examples of ineffective praise.

## Table 3
### Effective Positive Reinforcement is
### 1. Specific, 2. Verbal, 3. Positive, and 4. Genuine.

| Effective Positive Verbal Reinforcement | Ineffective Praise |
|---|---|
| • I really like the way you helped your sister clean up her toys. That is so kind of you. | • Great job! You're awesome! (*Not specific.*) |
| • Great job getting your chores done on your own initiative. You are becoming so responsible. | • I'm glad you finally got your chores done by yourself. (*Not positive.*) |
| • Thanks for taking out the trash, Sarah. I really appreciate your helpfulness. | • You're the best kid in the world! (*Not specific, not genuine.*) |
| • I know that you were upset because you didn't want to leave Amy's house. You did a good job leaving with me even when you didn't want to. | • You didn't cry and scream when we left. Good job! (*Not positive, calls attention to previous negative behavior.*) |
| • Good job using words instead of your hands, Tom. I know it's hard when you feel angry. Next time, I would like to see you try to say it calmly. | • Hey, stop yelling at him. At least you didn't hit him. (*Not positive, calls attention to previous negative behavior.*) |

When first using PVR, it is natural for parents to have questions and concerns regarding its administration, which we address below.

## Aren't we being manipulative when we use PVR?

Whether or not parents are using PVR, all parents are unwittingly and unintentionally manipulating their children to behave either appropriately or inappropriately. Any interaction you have with your children has an effect on how they will behave. With their own responses, most parents inadvertently promote conditions that make it easy for their children to choose negative behavior. You want to create interactions that make it easy for your children to choose appropriate behavior.

This is not to say that your children do not have free will. They are ultimately responsible for their choices. But we must remember that if making good choices is sometimes difficult for adults, it is even harder for children. Adults seeking to exercise, eat better, or give up destructive habits often need the camaraderie and support of friends or family to encourage these behavior changes. If the work that results in change is made to feel like drudgery and deprivation, it is natural for individuals to avoid it. But by making your children feel good about the positive changes they make, you are harnessing the tremendous energy that comes from their natural inclination to feel excited about success. Supporting children in making good choices is not manipulative, but an expression of your unconditional love.

## How do I use PVR at times when I don't feel like using it? Isn't that insincere?

It is imperative that your PVR be sincere and genuine. Children are extremely perceptive and can easily spot pho-niness or insincerity. But how do you express genuine PVR when you don't **feel** like expressing it, when in fact, you feel more like yelling at them? At times like these, you want to see your children in a different light. Remind yourself that children do not naturally know how to act appropriately. It is your job, as the adult, to teach them your values and ex-pectations for their behavior. While it may seem strange and insincere at times, as you practice PVR, it will begin to change the way you see your child. Though you want to be as genuine as possible, there is some truth to the saying, "Fake it till you make it." Sometimes the act of practicing a way of thinking allows you to internalize that way of think-ing.

## My children sometimes do nothing right. How can I PVR them at those times?

Sometimes it may be that your children are just having a bad day and you believe that nothing they do is commend-able. When you are feeling this way, you want to look for **any approximation** to the desired behavior in your children. In any given hour, there is almost always something positive your child does that you can pay attention to. Never mind that Brian took forty minutes to get dressed. When he finally does it, Mom does not point out the inordinate amount of time that he took to get it done. Instead, she says, "I like the way you got dressed on your own, Brian. You are learning to be responsible." If Abby has been throwing a tantrum for the last thirty minutes and finally stops, Dad can say, "I like that you calmed yourself down now." If Ellen has been yelling in the car, Mom can say, "I need you to use an inside voice in the car," and if Ellen does, Mom says, "Thank you for using an inside voice. It helps me keep us all safe in the car." By catching them doing something right, you will encourage and motivate them to do more.

## Will using PVR make our children dependent on praise to act appropriately?

Using PVR generally does not result in children being over-reliant on praise. Because PVR is specific, children will value the behavior and internalize its importance, then start repeating the behavior for its own value. As your children master the skill or value you want them to learn, you will find that they no longer need constant PVR to maintain it. You can then begin to gradually phase out the PVR for that mastered skill and move on to the next milestone in their growth toward maturity. Even after your child has mastered a task, if you find your child frequently asking, "Did you see me do such-and-such? Did I do a good job?" you may want to respond, "Yes, I did! I like that you remembered to turn off your light without being told. I bet you feel good about yourself for remembering too!" In this way, you can guide your children to learn to be proud of their own growth.

You can also begin phasing out PVR by encouraging

your children to enjoy the benefits of their newly mastered behavior. "I bet it feels great to have your homework out of the way. Now you can just relax and play without feeling nervous," or "Your room is so clean and beautiful! It feels so nice to be in it. I am guessing you like it too." As your children begin to enjoy the benefits of the behavior, they will become less reliant on getting attention for it.

Although phasing out PVR is a good way to help children learn to be independent, this does not mean you should never use them for mastered tasks. "John, I am so proud of you for all the ways you've become so mature. You've worked hard on controlling your emotions and being flexible and gracious with others, and it shows." When you point out how much your children have grown in certain characteristics, you not only help maintain those characteristics, but you empower your children for future growth. You teach your children that with a little hard work, they can successfully master any change in behavior.

## Will using PVR make our children too soft to deal with the real world?

There is nothing more powerful than equipping our children with the armor of unconditional love to help them withstand the negativity of "the real world." When children are secure in the knowledge that they are loved, appreciated, and taught well through their parents, they have the confidence to weather the negative storms of the world. Children will unfortunately have plenty of opportunity to deal with harshness and criticism in their lives. The world of the family, which is no less "real" to them, should not be a place that adds more harshness and criticism. Instead, it should be a place to recharge, a place to learn appropriate behavior in a safe and loving environment, and a place to learn to deal with the negative influences of the world. It is our job to support them as they navigate through situations, to teach them appropriate and mature responses in a way that helps them become independent. Positive parenting, strong values, and high expectations will equip them to take on life's challenges with confidence.

In later chapters, we will discuss other tools for addressing your children's inappropriate behaviors, such as logical consequences and setting appropriate boundaries. We are introducing PVR first because we want to stress its importance. PVR is the crux of positive behavior support. With practice, you can make it automatic in your parenting because it is the most effective way to change behavior. When used in tandem with clear expectations, listening, ignoring, and other skills that will be discussed in later chapters, PVR will dramatically change the behavior of your children, and create a home environment of care, support, and encouragement.

## Exercise II

Change each of the statements below into a specific PVR.

1. Good job! (Child gets homework done independently.)
   Change to:

   _____

   _____

   _____


2. You did not strike out in the game. I am proud of you.
   Change to:

   _____

   _____

   _____


3. You are such a big boy now! (Child puts on shoes.)
   Change to:

   _____

   _____

   _____

## Exercise III

In Chapter One, we asked you to consider the most challenging behaviors that you observed in your children. Now we will review that behavior and analyze its purpose and the reinforcement (positive or negative) that it received.

### Targeted Behavior:

| What did your child do or not do? | What might be your child's purpose? | How was the behavior reinforced? | What behavioral change can I make? |
|---|---|---|---|
|  |  |  |  |

### Chapter Two Summary

- All behavior is purposeful. Children act in specific ways for specific reasons, not because they are being bad, but because they achieve something by behaving the way they do.
- Any behavior that is given positive or negative attention will increase. Positive behavior increases with positive attention. Negative behavior increases with positive **or negative** attention.

- Behavior change first begins with the parents, not the children. Repeating the same response tends to create the same behavior. If we want our children to change, we must first change ourselves.
- The most effective way to reduce problem behavior is to positively reinforce desirable behavior through the use of specific, genuine, positive verbal affirmation (**Positive Verbal Reinforcement**).

## Chapter Three

........................................

# MAKE IT EASY FOR
# KIDS TO BEHAVE

## Setting Clear Expectations, Values, and Structure

*Let no unwholesome word proceed from your mouth, but only such a word as is good for edification according to the need of the moment, so that it will give grace to those who hear. Do not grieve the Holy Spirit of God, by whom you were sealed for the day of redemption. Let all bitterness and wrath and anger and clamor and slander be put away from you, along with all malice. Be kind to one another, tender-hearted, forgiving each other, just as God in Christ also has forgiven you.*

*—Ephesians 4:29-32, NASB*

The scripture from the Apostle Paul's letter to the Ephesians sets his entire chapter within its theological context. Although Paul formulates some of his instructions in what we might call a negative framework, he does not do so without stating what the positive outcome would be. "Let no unwholesome word proceed from your mouth" is tempered with "but only such a word that is good for edification." We are to be "kind to one another, tender-hearted, forgiving...etc." God calls us to live as one who exhorts and encourages others.

Most likely we understand these words in the framework of our adult interactions, but fail to see them as meaningful in relationships with our children. What would happen if all "anger and clamor and slander" were "put away" from interactions with our children? Wouldn't we be a step closer to becoming the kind of parent God is to us?

In the last chapter, we had the opportunity to analyze a problem behavior in light of the three basic principles of positive behavior support. You might be thinking, "This may work for certain difficulties, but I don't have the time to analyze every inappropriate behavior that occurs throughout the day. I want my child to behave more appropriately all the time without having to constantly analyze what is going on and how to change it." This chapter will help you proactively teach your child to behave well before negative behavior occurs.

A large part of the *Keep It Positive* method is prevention: preventing negative behavior from happening. The idea is to **proactively teach** good behavior instead of **reactively punishing** unwanted behavior. In this chapter, we will discuss how to structure a positive environment where appropriate behavior is encouraged and inappropriate behavior is discouraged. You will learn how to develop family values and expectations that all family members are expected to uphold. You will also learn how to structure your household to help your children know what to expect, which will help them act accordingly. In this environment, you will come to value each person's contributions to the family unit, showing your children that you are learning, practicing, and growing along with them.

---

**Teach Clear, Positive Expectations and Give Structure**

Why?

- We all do better when we know exactly what is expected of us.

- It positions children to behave successfully.

Then, give Positive Verbal Reinforcement (PVR)

---

Instead of creating an atmosphere of reaction, rejection, and negative interaction, we want to create an environment of peaceful, loving, positive support with clear expectations. You may be thinking, "I already have clear expectations. I expect my children to mind me, I expect them to not hit each other, and I expect them to not talk back when I tell them to do something." Think about how these expectations are taught to children. In the vast majority of cases, they are usually not taught at all. Children are usually expected to "know" what is right by verbal interactions that come only when they do something wrong.

Remember that negative, reactive teaching is proven to be much less effective than positive, proactive teaching. Of the three expectations described above, "to mind me, to not hit, not talk back," which is a positive expectation? Clearly only the first one is positive. The other two are negative expectations. "What is wrong with that?" you may ask. "I want my children to know that there are certain things that are wrong."

While we do want our children to learn right from wrong, negative expectations are not an effective way to accomplish that purpose. Why? One reason is that we can never create enough negative expectations to address every behavior that our child may attempt. Just try to imagine the situations:

1. Don't hit your sister.
2. Don't hit your brother (not covered in No. 1).
3. Don't push your sister.
4. Don't push your brother (Nos. 3 & 4 not covered in Nos. 1 & 2).
5. Don't scream at your parents.
6. Don't spit.
7. Don't talk back to your parents.
8. Don't run in the house.
9. Don't throw your toys.
10. Don't leave when I am talking to you.

In these ten examples of negative expectations, you can see that we have barely scratched the surface of all the things you may not want your children to do. Prohibitions are endless.

Prohibitions will not achieve the long-term goal—to have your children internalize important social values and act accordingly. This is true for adults as well. Imagine if your boss at work constantly pointed out what you were doing wrong and only told you what not to do. Would these interactions help your motivation, drive, and creativity? More often than not, children learn our expectations only when they fail to meet them because our expectations are un-known or unclear.

We deepen the problem by blaming our children when they fail to meet expectations we never clearly communi-cated. Many adults mature with similar habits. They often expect spouses, colleagues, and friends to "read their minds." For both children and adults, reactive responses are no substitute for clearly communicated expectations.

Prohibitions are also ineffective because they create a hostile relationship between you and your children. Con-stant reprimands and negative, frustrated reactions—even from loving, well-meaning parents—can be degrading and hurtful, instilling anger and resentment in children. Like adults, children tend to behave better when they feel that they can be successful, and constant reprimands tend to squelch the desire of children to do the right thing.

Clear expectations are not about what you don't want your children to do. They are about what you want your chil-dren **to** do. You want your children to be kind, responsible, and respectful to others. Clear expectations reflect the values that you treasure and want your children to internalize.

As you will see, this does not mean that you should never tell children what not to do. There is a time and place for clear prohibitions, especially when an immediate health or safety issue arises. But in all cases, you must be careful to approach your children with kindness and love, in a prob-lem-solving rather than in a judgmental manner if you ex-pect to be heard. Always use problems as opportunities to teach, not to punish.

The following steps will help you and your family focus on the positive expectations you have for your children:

1. Create a list of your **family values** and teach what they mean.

2. Establish and teach your age-appropriate **expectations for particular tasks**.

3. Always reinforce desired behavior with positive verbal reinforcement (**PVR**).

4. Create **structure** and **routines** to help make desired behavior automatic.

## 1. Create a List of Your Family Values and Teach What They Mean

The first step toward developing positive expectations with your children is to make a list of three to five broad values that will apply to everyone in the family. If your children are five years old or younger, you can develop the values yourself and then teach them to your children. If your children are at least six years old, you can guide them in developing the values along with you. Choose a time when your children are content, well fed, energetic, and positive. Do not start the process after they have been reprimanded or have been fighting with each other.

Keep the conversation positive. Tell your children that

together, you are going to make a list of values that everyone in the house will do their best to follow. Explain that values are like big rules that everyone should follow, such as "Be kind to one another." Then ask your children to come up with some of their own. Most likely, their rules will be stated in the negative, for example, "Don't hit." They will need your direction to rephrase their ideas in the positive. For example, "Touch only with kindness," and eventually, "Be kind." Write each down and see if you can condense them into three to five values. Many will be similar to each other and fall under one umbrella value. The following is an example of four positively stated values that can cover just about all the negative expectations you can imagine.

1. Be kind to one another.
2. Be a helper.
3. Be responsible.
4. Be a good listener.

Write the words large enough to be seen from afar and post the list where all can see it, on the refrigerator or a wall in the family room, for example. If you have any non-readers, draw iconic illustrations, or attach photographs of your children acting out those values. You may even stress the importance of these values and make it fun for young children by labeling your list "Smith Family Treasures," for example. Children will know that in your family, these values will be treasured more than gold.

Once you have determined your family's values, you will

want to teach them in a way that your children will understand. This involves sitting down with your children for the
specific purpose of pleasantly, specifically, and concretely
teaching what each value means. For example, one family
who adopted this process selected the following positive
family values:

1.  Treat each other with love.
2.  Keep each other safe.
3.  Listen to each other.

After they selected the above values, a family meeting
was convened to teach them to their five-year-old twins.
Mom and Dad talked about what each value meant and
play-acted the examples. Then they asked their children to
make up their own examples of the values. For example,
"What does it look like when we treat each other with love?"
They also went through examples of the opposite. "What
does it look like when we don't treat each other with love?"
Both parents then committed themselves to positive verbal
reinforcement of any approximate behavior in line with their
family values. The atmosphere in the home was greatly im-
proved.

The direct instruction method generally achieves the
most success in the positive behavioral support model, but
there are numerous supplemental ways to teach children
your family values. Reading children's books together, role
playing, puppets, public television shows, carefully selected
movies, and of course, life events can provide a plethora of

ethical dilemmas, morals, and values to discuss with your children.

The important thing to remember when teaching is to avoid lecturing. Lectures do not generally work, but you can guide your children to draw the right conclusions. When they find out what the "right thing" is, it will be not only because Mom and Dad have told them, but also because they believe it to be so. The value will be theirs forever because they have taken part in discovering it with your guidance.

## 2. Establish and Teach Your Age-Appropriate Expectations for Particular Tasks

After you teach your broad family values, you also want to teach your expectations for particular tasks—such as cleaning up, brushing teeth, or completing homework—in a clear, specific, and positive way. Again, choose a time to teach when your children are in a good mood, not right after they have done something wrong. When first implementing this program, you may want to focus on one or two tasks for your child to work on until your child has mastered that skill.

> *Teach your expectations for particular tasks in a clear, specific, and **positive** way.*

For example, Jeannie, one of the parents in our class, was frustrated with her daughter, Sara, for leaving her backpack on the floor, in the car, and in the garage, and she hated having to reprimand Sara about it several times a day. After learning to set clear expectations, Jeannie went home and did the following. On Sunday night, when Sara was in a good mood, Jeannie said, "Sara, you are growing up now and taking care of your things so well. I would like you to be responsible with your backpack too. When you get home from school tomorrow, I expect you to bring your backpack in, take out your lunch bag and papers, and put them on the counter. Then, hang your backpack on the hook. Can you tell me what I want you to do with your backpack after school?" Sara repeated what she heard. "Good job listening, Sara! Let's practice it right now." (Practicing the skill right then helps to reinforce the action and makes sure she understands the expectation.) "Great job remembering and following directions. I know you'll do a terrific job tomorrow too."

After Sara was informed of the expectation in a positive way, she began to bring in her backpack more often. When Sara remembered on her own, Jeannie would say, "I like the way you put away your backpack before being told. Thank you for remembering."

If you develop a policy of always making your expectations clear and then positively reinforcing them when those expectations are met, you give your children the opportunity to do the **right** thing and a chance to be rewarded not only with your praise, but also with the internal pride and satisfaction of a job well done. Of course, one practice session followed by consistent PVR may not be enough for Sara to remember consistently. In Chapter Four, we will discuss some additional strategies to support your child in learning a skill.

> *Make sure your expectations are age and developmentally appropriate.*

When you set specific expectations for particular tasks, make sure your expectations are age and developmentally appropriate. While it is appropriate to expect an eight-year-old to clean up his toys independently, pour water without spilling, or eat without leaving crumbs, it is not appropriate to expect a four-year-old to do the same. Keep in mind the developmental growth and limitations of your children and pick learning goals that match your child's development.

Many parents become stymied when they expect their children to respond to expectations that are not age or developmentally appropriate. One parent shared this story. Mom and Dad were enjoying a beautiful, sunny day as they waited to be served Sunday brunch at a restaurant. Their three-year-old daughter, Annika, began to play with the salt and pepper shakers, then started entertaining herself with the sugar packets on the table. Her mom told her to stop that activity. The mom then indicated that after sitting for a while, without provocation, Annika put her head down on the table and began to sob. The mother was puzzled. Why would her daughter be so upset when they were enjoying such a nice day eating out?

In this situation, what may be enjoyable for us as adults (relaxing and waiting for our food to be served on a beautiful day) can be interminably boring for a three-year-old. It is hard for a three-year-old to sit with nothing to do, and it is an unrealistic expectation to think that a three-year-old would enjoy just sitting.

Instead, Mom can say, "Annika, when we get to the restaurant this morning, we may have to wait awhile for our food. Let's bring a backpack with some things you can do while we wait." Annika can help select things for the backpack, such as crayons and a coloring book or a small toy. At the restaurant Mom can encourage Annika by saying, "I like how patiently you are waiting for your breakfast." In this manner, Annika's mother can set clear expectations for a particular task and use PVR to reinforce appropriate behavior.

It is also easy to forget that children find it hard to do simple tasks that we adults can do easily. In an attempt to teach the importance of helpfulness and a good work ethic, Mom asks Beth, her four-year-old, to put all of her clothes in the hamper daily for the laundry. While Beth may at times get all of her clothes in the hamper, it is reasonable to expect that she may miss some of them. What if Mom chastises her by saying, "Beth, you missed your socks in the living room. I asked you to get all of your clothes in the hamper, and you are not getting it done. You cannot play outside until this work is finished." How might Beth feel in this situation? She will probably be discouraged and unmotivated to complete this task.

Instead, Mom can encourage her by saying, "I like how you picked up your pajamas and put them in the hamper. You are being so helpful and learning how to put all your clothes in the hamper." Instead of pointing out the missing socks, Mom is encouraging Beth's helpfulness by noticing what she did right. If you encourage your children when they accomplish a task instead of pointing out their short-comings, the likelihood of their improving their performance on such tasks becomes much greater.

Understanding the developmental level of your children can help you better understand their behavior and have clear expectations that they can meet. Although it would be too lengthy to discuss all of the developmental levels of children here, there are many experts on children's development that you can read for greater understanding. Two that we will mention are Jean Piaget and Erik Erikson. There are also many websites that can provide easily accessible information on this topic.

> *Follow your own family values*
> *when you discipline.*

One of the most powerful and most effective ways to teach your children your values is to practice them yourself. You must endeavor to act according to your values, not only with others, but also with your children. The common saying, "Do as I say, not as I do," is a reminder of the absurdity of an approach based on hypocrisy.

Children are extremely perceptive and highly impressionable. They do as we **do**, not as we say. Parents are often shocked and upset to find that the same negative words they use sometimes come out of their own children's mouths. When we are harsh and unforgiving with our children, they learn to be harsh and unforgiving with others, with us, and, ultimately, with themselves.

So if you want your children to say please and thank you, you need to model politeness by consistently using the same polite words with them. If you want your children to learn to control their emotions, you need to control your own emotions even when you are angered by their immaturity or irritating behavior. Is this hard to do? Definitely. Parenting is one of the most challenging jobs in the world because it is hard not to take children's misbehavior personally. Our own children can test the limits of our patience, our resilience, and our resolve in ways that no other children can. But because of these very challenges, parenting is also a gift that provides a wealth of opportunity for our own growth, through the trials and rewards we experience with our children.

> *Share your mistakes with your children; apologize when you make mistakes. They will respect and trust you more.*

Doing your best to uphold your family values does not mean that you have to be perfect. Parenting is difficult, and you will make mistakes, but children are resilient and can also be forgiving. By doing your best to be kind to your children even when you are stretched to your limits, you model how to deal with difficult situations. By apologizing when you make mistakes, and forgiving your children when they are sorry, you model forgiveness, humility, and grace.

*Scotty's Idea of Perfect*

*When Rose's son, Scotty, was five, she used time-outs for all kinds of negative behavior. Scotty was exhausted and discouraged from trying so hard to meet her negatively administered expectations. One day, sobbing, frustrated, and discouraged, Scotty cried, "Mommy, it's so hard for me! I'm not perfect like you or Daddy!"*

*Rose says, "I was shocked that he thought we were perfect. I knew I must have made the mistake of letting him think I was. From his point of view, I was always right. I had told him the right ways I deal with things, but I had never told him how many mistakes I often make. I never apologized when I lost my temper because I believed it was usually his fault. But after learning the Keep It Positive method, I changed how I related with him. Now he knows that Mommy is not perfect. He respects and trusts me more because I share my mistakes with him. He is no longer under pressure to be perfect, and realizes that all of us, as a family, are working toward becoming better together."*

## 3. Always Reinforce Desired Behavior with Positive Verbal Reinforcement (PVR)

Even after you have taught your children your clear expectations, remember that they are still children and need your support to learn to be disciplined enough to follow through. As you know, just because children know what to do, that doesn't mean they will start doing it automatically. Children are, by definition, immature, and they need our guidance to learn to behave appropriately and to fight the urge to behave inappropriately.

A beginning teacher, frustrated with her third-grade class, once cried, "You need to stop acting like children!" Bewildered, the kids looked at one another and then at her and said, "But Mrs. Jones, we ARE children!" She paused, laughed, and said, "Yes, of course you are!" Children do not instinctively know how to control themselves, and it is unfair to expect them to without giving them some support. It is also unfair to expect them to learn by berating them or by constantly telling them what not to do.

So how do you support them? The best way is with Positive Verbal Reinforcement (PVR). We will discuss other ways, such as logical consequences, in later chapters, but PVR should always be your primary action. Whenever you see your child act in accordance with any of the values and expectations you have made clear, you want to provide positive reinforcement.

As discussed in Chapter Two, all four elements of reinforcement are important. Your statement should be 1) Specific, 2) Verbal, 3) Positive, and 4) Genuine. If your son brushes his teeth without a struggle, you can say, "I like how you brushed your teeth by yourself so quickly. You are being so responsible!" Linking the action to one of your family values (being responsible) highlights the general value you want your child to internalize.

You can also proactively encourage positive behavior by saying, "John, I know you can be responsible and brush your teeth quickly so we can get to school on time." Then, when he does, you say, "I like how you went right to brushing so quickly. You're being so responsible!" Frequent and specific verbal reinforcement of your children's positive actions is a simple way to create the expectation of positive behavior. In this way, you will encourage your children to repeat that responsible act—and if you stay positive, they **will** repeat it.

> *Stay positive. Pointing out negative behavior every time your child veers away from your family values will negate the effectiveness of the values.*

When relating your expectations and values, it is essential that you do not begin to use them in a negative way. Say John grabs Mary's toy while they are playing. Mom says, "John, don't grab Mary's toy, that is not kind!" John already knows that his behavior is not kind because he has been **taught** this when the family values were developed. Pointing out noncompliance is negative reinforcement, which encourages John to repeat the behavior. Unless you are confronted with a health and safety issue, it is best to ignore the behavior. Remember that any attention paid to negative behavior tends to cause the behavior to increase.

Positive support needs to stay positive. Pointing out negative behavior is counterproductive. The purpose of your family values and expectations is to provide all family members with guidelines for how to behave. The values and expectations are not to be used as a stick to be brandished every time your children veer off course. If used this way, they will soon lose their effectiveness. Children may then begin to view them negatively as just another set of rules they cannot master. Be patient while your children learn. Remember as with adults, it is frustrating and discouraging for children when they are expected to behave perfectly in achieving a goal.

## 4. Create a Structured Environment to Help Make Desired Behavior Automatic

Structure exists in every predictable environment. In the workplace, companies write vision statements to inspire employees and focus their direction. Routines, procedures, and job descriptions help employees know what is expected of them. We all do better in our workplaces, in stores, on the road, in theaters, in churches, and in most any situation when we know how things work and exactly what is expected of us.

> *Structure and routines help make appropriate behavior automatic. We all do better when we know what is expected of us.*

Children are no different. In fact, they especially thrive in structured, predictable environments. When your children know what is expected of them and what routines to follow, they will be more likely to meet your expectations. Structure and routines give them a sense of stability and security, and help them to successfully meet the positive expectations you have established.

Structure should always be developed within the parameters of your family values. Once your family's expectations are clear, you can develop the structure to help implement those expectations. Structure is very important as it pertains to bedtime, mealtime, playtime, and personal hygiene. As children get older, structured expectations will include different areas such as homework, chores, television time, and extracurricular activities. Who, what, when, where, and how will be the questions you will be answering for your children when you provide structure for these activities.

Suppose you want to teach your children to "be helpers" or to "be responsible" by putting away their toys when they are done playing. If you have specific places where the toys belong and a specific time of day that your children are expected to clean up, then you are providing the structure that allows your child to meet your expectations.

Before a particular event, you can share your planned schedule and your behavioral expectations so your children can be successful. Let's say your five-year-old daughter, Kelly, has a playdate with her friend Susie at your house. Before Susie arrives, tell Kelly your behavioral expectations and your schedule. By providing your child with both of these things, you make clear the structure for the event. "I am so happy that Susie is coming over to play today. You and Susie can play with your toys for one hour and then we will all pick them up together."

While Kelly and Susie are playing, you do not give them

any reminders about cleaning up. Reminders send a hidden message that you don't think your children will meet your expectations. Saying, "Don't forget that you will have to pick up the toys later," communicates, "I do not think that you listen to me," or "I am nervous about you cleaning up, and I'm not sure that you will do it." Instead, when the play hour is up, you say, "It's time to clean up. Let's pick up the toys together."

If you catch anyone putting away a toy independently, you say in a quiet way, "I like how you are being a helper by cleaning up the toys" (PVR). The message is that a five-year-old needs assistance to complete this job successfully, you are there to help her be successful, and you appreciate her efforts. What a wonderful message to give your child.

> *Do not give reminders. Reminders send a hidden message that you don't think your child will meet your expectations.*

Consider the opposite scenario. Susie comes over, but Kelly has not been informed of any expectations. After an hour of playtime, Mom comes in and says, "Time to put away the toys. Susie has to go home." Mom is surprising the girls with the unpalatable task of cleaning up, which adds to the frustration of having to end the playdate. The likelihood of their jumping in to pick up toys is slim.

Mom reminds them, "I told you to put away the toys, and you have not picked up anything," which is often followed by, "Next time, I don't know if Susie can come over to play if you cannot clean up your toys." The message here is that Kelly will be punished by something that is unrelated to her behavior. Kelly did not expect to have to put away toys, and she does not see how failing to do so should mean that she will not see Susie again. Kelly then begins to see Mom's expectations and punishments as capricious and random. As the child continues to avoid the task, the situation can escalate to greater negative interaction or more severe punishment from the parent. While her mom's expectation is exactly the same in both scenarios, Kelly's is not, which is why the second scenario positions her for failure. Instead of creating a situation that is ripe for failure, you want to provide your child with a platform for success.

In developing routines and structures, you must also take into account your family's schedule and your home environment. There is not only one "right" structure, and routines will not work if they are not tailored to meet the unique needs of both parents and children. For example, a habitual late bedtime for a toddler may make it difficult for him to behave the next day. So the bedtime may need to be rethought. Or a homework time scheduled right after school without some downtime may be too difficult to manage for some children. So, for example, an afterschool snack or a quick run around the block before homework is begun could be built into the routine.

Jerry is an example of a parent who changed a bedtime routine in a thoughtful way to encourage success. Six-year-old Trevor has trouble with his bedtime routine. He dawdles when it's time to get ready for bed, gets distracted with his toys, or plays with his younger sister. His father, Jerry, is tired of asking him over and over to brush his teeth, take a bath, etc. When Trevor finally does get ready for bed, he insists on finishing his book at reading time, or insists on more books or a longer snuggle, pushing his actual bedtime later and later.

Jerry wants to provide structure to help Trevor be successful. He arranges a routine in which Trevor picks up his toys before dinner so he is not tempted to play and dawdle after dinner. Then Jerry says, "Trevor, after dinner, I expect you to take a bath, brush your teeth, and put on your pajamas. When you are done, I will read with you until eight o'clock. When you are ready for bed, we will have time to read, but all reading will stop at eight. I am looking forward to reading with you, and I know you will do a good job getting ready so we can have more time to read."

In this way, Jerry builds a logical consequence of dawdling into the routine, which is running out of time to read. (Using logical consequences to address inappropriate behavior will be further discussed in Chapter Four.) Because Jerry has told Trevor the details of the new bedtime routine in advance, Trevor has the opportunity to meet Jerry's clear expectations. Moreover, Trevor has a parent who is rooting for him to be successful. When Trevor does take a bath, Jerry gives him PVR, and for a while, Jerry continues to provide PVR for every step in the process.

What does Jerry do when Trevor avoids getting ready? He ignores it, but allows the pre-stated consequence to happen. Calmly, he says, "It's time for bed. I will tuck you in and say good night." When Trevor rebels at the new rule, insisting on reading a book, Jerry calmly states, "I'm disappointed, too, that we can't read. I really enjoy reading with you. I'm sure tomorrow you'll be quicker and we'll have lots of time to read."

Notice that this is not the same as saying, "Well, if you had just gotten ready on time, we could have read. Next time, do a better job." This statement is critical and does not motivate or encourage Trevor to do better. Instead, the message should be that Jerry is genuinely disappointed because he enjoys reading with his son and that Jerry genuinely believes that Trevor is capable of making good choices.

Another tool we recommend to help young children follow time structures and prevent dawdling is the visual timer. Unlike a ringing timer, a visual timer displays a red triangle that shrinks as time passes, giving children a graphic representation of the time left to complete an activity. When paired with clear expectations and no reminders, a visual timer can be useful to help children complete a task, such as going to bed, getting dressed, or getting out the door on time. Because most young children do not have a clear understanding of time and its passage, it is often ineffective to say, "You have ten minutes left," or "We are leaving at 8:30," but even young children can see the amount of time left on a visual timer.

When introducing the timer to your child, keep it positive. "Max, I bought you this neat timer to help you know how much time you have left to finish something or get ready to go." Then, explain how it works. By empowering children to be able to see how much time they have left for themselves, you are shifting the responsibility for keeping track of the time from yourself to your children. More information about the visible timer is included in "A Final Note from the Authors" at the end of this book.

> *Be consistent with routines, while allowing for some flexibility when needed.*

Once you develop structures and routines, it is best to try to remain consistent with them, allowing for some flexibility as needed. Consistency gives children the stability they need to feel secure with your expectations. When children successfully follow the established structure, you should always positively recognize and support their actions.

This does not mean that you should rigidly program your children by the clock. While you want to do your part to help your children follow established routines, it is best not to make a big deal about a child's failure to comply. Remember, negative attention paid to unwanted behavior increases the unwanted behavior. The purpose of structure is to provide a positive environment that encourages your children to be successful.

Another way to provide structure is to set up your children's physical environment to help them be successful. If you want to facilitate good study habits, make sure your children have a clean, quiet environment to do their homework. If you want your four-year-old to stop using the scissors to cut her hair and various objects in your house, put the scissors in a place where she cannot see or reach them. Then supervise her activities when she is using them, giving PVR when she uses them appropriately. If you want your child to stop sneaking cookies from the cookie jar, put them up high in a place where they are not visible. If you want your older child to come home at a certain hour, give him a watch so he can keep track of the time. The visible timer is another example of setting up structure. By setting up the environment to avoid giving undue temptation and to facilitate compliance, you make it easier for your children to be successful.

## Exercise IV

Develop your Family Values (expectations of positive behavior) and specifically teach them to your children. Record what happens.

### Your Family Values

_____

_____

_____

_____

_____

_____

## Chapter Three Summary

Create an environment conducive to positive behavior with the following steps:

- Set clear, positive expectations at the macro level (family values):
    o Develop family values.
    o Specifically teach family values.
    o **PVR.**
- Set clear, positive expectations at the micro level (specific skills, tasks):
    o Develop clear procedures and tasks.
    o Specifically teach the skills.
    o Practice the skills with your children.
    o **PVR any approximation to the appropriate behavior.**
- Make sure your expectations are developmentally appropriate.
- Follow your own family values when you parent and when you discipline.
- Provide structure and routine to promote successful compliance.
- Be patient with children as they learn, and do not expect instant results.

......................................

## Chapter Four

# WHAT TO DO WHEN YOUR CHILD MISBEHAVES

## Tools for Responding to Inappropriate Behavior

*What happened was this: People knew God perfectly well, but when they didn't treat him like God, refusing to worship him, they trivialized themselves into silliness and confusion so that there was neither sense nor direction left in their lives. They pretended to know it all, but were illiterate regarding life. They traded the glory of God who holds the whole world in his hands for cheap figurines you can buy at any roadside stand. So God said, in effect, "If that's what you want, that's what you get." It wasn't long before they were living in a pigpen, smeared with filth, filthy inside and out. And all this because they traded the true God for a fake god, and worshiped the god they made instead of the God who made them—the God we bless, the God who blesses us. Oh, yes!*

—The Message, *inspired by Romans 1:21-25*

On the surface, the opening passage looks a bit callous, cold, and well, a bit out of place in a book on positive parenting. But try to look beneath the simple words to see the truth within them. We often underestimate the freedom that God gives human beings. When people refuse what God is trying to do, their "punishment" is nothing more than the consequences of their actions. In this case, the Apostle Paul is describing the prevalence of idolatry in Roman society. Rather than becoming punitive, God expresses love in the freedoms we are given. Instead of seeing individuals as just evil and bad, God sees us for who we can become. When we make choices to act contrary to who we really ARE, God sends no terrible punishment or a "time-out." God simply lets the consequences of our actions—which ultimately harm only ourselves—happen. God shows the way. There are signs directing us, but we must choose the path to follow. Each of us is responsible for our actions, not God. But God, like the perfect parent, does not punish, rather He invites us into a new way of living in which we can experience the life we were always meant to have.

In the last chapter, we discussed how to create an environment of positive support for all family members by creating a list of family values. We also shared how to encourage appropriate behavior, set age-appropriate expectations, teach them specifically, and provide structure and routine to facilitate success. When beginning the *Keep It Positive* methodology, most parents find it easy to positively reinforce their child's good behavior, but may feel somewhat stumped when trying to manage inappropriate behavior. Parents often ask, "What do we do when our children are misbehaving? Can we use consequences? Are time-outs okay? Can we ever say 'No, don't do such and such'? What do we do when our children are noncompliant or outright defiant? What do we do when our children hit, lie, scream, or whine?"

The *Keep It Positive* method includes powerful tools to respond to inappropriate behavior. While many of these tools will seem familiar to you, the key difference of each is in the **way** each tool is implemented. They are always administered in a firm, but loving way, with patience and respect for your child. Although some of these tools will sound similar to punishments, we do not categorize them as such because we do not administer them in a punitive fashion. Remember that punitive methods are not effective for long-term change.

When a child behaves inappropriately, you can use one or a combination of the tools in Table 4 to respond to the behavior. They are listed in order of effectiveness. The most effective tool is, of course, Positive Verbal Reinforcement, as discussed in Chapters Two and Three, and we encourage you to re-read these sections. Coupling PVR with the other tools in this chapter will make those other tools exponentially more effective. Always keep in mind your child's age and developmental level when using these tools.

**Table 4**

**Positive Behavior Support Tools**

| Range of Effectiveness | Tool |
|---|---|
| More Effective<br><br>Less Effective | • **Positive Verbal Reinforcement (PVR)**<br>Should always be a part of your daily routine.<br>Should always be coupled with any other tools used.<br><br>• **Ignore Inappropriate Behavior**<br>After setting clear expectations and boundaries.<br>Use limited interactions for health and safety issues.<br><br>• **Natural Consequences**<br><br>• **Predetermined Consequences**<br>Must be stated in advance. |

In the discussion of the tools that follow, we use examples to illustrate the way the tools can be used. These examples are by no means a complete list of all the situations in which these tools can be used. Because there is no limit to the type and number of situations that can present themselves, we focus not on providing the means of dealing with every specific behavior, but on the use of the methodology. When you understand the methodology and underlying concepts, you can apply these techniques to any behavior your child exhibits, using your own expert knowledge of your child and of the situation at hand.

## Ignoring Negative Behavior
## (After Clear Expectations and Boundaries)

Remember that any attention paid to negative behavior will increase that behavior. So when a child acts inappropriately, you should pay no attention to the behavior. Consequently, the behavior will decrease. It sounds too simple doesn't it? Yet ignoring unwanted behavior is one of the most powerful tools in this methodology. When a child gets no reaction for negative behavior, the child gets nothing out of it, so after an initial escalation of the behavior, the behavior will decrease.

Ignoring negative behavior is one of your most powerful strategies, but also one that takes a good deal of determination and patience to use. Because it goes against the conventional wisdom, "If a child misbehaves, the parent should punish her or **do** something to stop it," parents often feel pressured to do something rather than nothing. When you ignore, however, you are saying something more powerful than anything you could say with words. Through your momentary inaction, you are effectively saying to your child, "The behavior you are engaging in is not appropriate, and you will get no attention from me for doing it." Conversely, when the child ceases the negative behavior, you will notice it and encourage it with PVR. This sends the message, "When you behave well, it will be noticed and encouraged, and I will pay attention to it." As will be discussed later, you will also be setting expectations and boundaries, and teaching outside of the moment of misbehavior.

Consider a common scenario. Little Lauren is screaming and crying at the grocery store. Suppose Lauren's mom says, "Lauren, if you stop screaming, Mommy will buy you a piece of candy." Will this work? Most probably, yes! But what will happen the next time they are in the store? Lauren will begin screaming again to get that piece of candy. Mom has just given Lauren a reason to scream the next time she doesn't get her way. Lauren thinks, "If I scream, I might get a piece of candy!" Mom has positively reinforced the negative behavior.

Suppose Mom continues to buy the candy each time, but then finally gets fed up with the screaming and puts her foot down. "I am not buying you any candy because you keep on screaming and crying in the store. I'm so sick of this! Stop crying now!" Now Mom is doing the screaming. She has modeled the very behavior she wants to eliminate. Mom has also made it more likely that Lauren will behave this way again because she has reacted to Lauren's misbehavior. Mom has now negatively reinforced a negative behavior.

What does the scenario look like if Mom uses the strategy of ignoring under the *Keep It Positive* method? Mom pairs her ignoring strategy with clear expectations and boundaries.

Even before Mom enters the store, she gives Lauren her clear expectations as discussed in Chapter Three. Mom says, "We are going to go to the store to buy a few things. I know that it is hard to be patient, but when you listen to Mommy, it helps me to get finished quickly. I know you can sit nicely and be patient while we are there." If Mom has reinforced crying over candy in the past, she can also pair this with a clear boundary. "We will not buy treats or candy in the store today."

While she is in the store, Mom **frequently** notices and gives PVR to any approximation to appropriate behavior. "Thank you for sitting quietly in the cart, Lauren. It's so nice to have you along," "I like how you're waiting patiently while I pick out the things we need," and "You are doing such a good job staying in your seat. I like that you are staying safe." Mom also keeps Lauren engaged as she shops, talking about the various items she picks out, to keep it a pleasant experience for both of them. With PVR and clear expectations, Mom is teaching Lauren appropriate behavior while shopping.

Suppose even with all of Mom's clear expectations and PVR, Lauren gets a little wiggly in the cart. Mom ignores this and keeps shopping. Lauren starts to cry. Mom ignores this too. Lauren starts to whine that she wants to buy a toy. Mom says just once, in a quiet voice, "We already said that we are not going to buy any candy or toys today." When Lauren increases her crying and whining, Mom does not further engage with her in any way and continues to ignore. As she goes through the checkout line, Lauren starts screaming.

Mom ignores the screaming, completes her purchases, and leaves the store. Will Lauren stop crying immediately? Probably not the first time, but what incentive is there for Lauren to cry the next time she is in the store? By not giving in to Lauren's behavior with attention, candy, or toys, Mom is teaching her that her boundaries are not flexible. Lauren will learn that whining and screaming will not get her what she wants.

## The Extinction Burst — It gets worse before it gets better.

Lauren's initial negative reaction to Mom's persistent ignoring is typical to that of most children. When you ignore negative behavior, that behavior will often get worse before it gets better. In behavioral terminology, this escalation of negative behavior is called an **extinction burst**. Before the unwanted behavior goes away, or becomes extinct, it reaches a peak, called a burst. The intensity and duration of the extinction burst will vary depending on how often and how strongly the behavior was previously reinforced.

Because Lauren is used to getting what she wants by screaming, the behavior is harder to extinguish. Lauren subconsciously thinks, "This has worked before, but it's not working this time. I need to do it louder and longer to make it work." Lauren's thinking is not manipulative. It is a product of the knowledge that her inappropriate behavior gains access to something, and she wants that something again, right now!

So when Mom gives Lauren clear expectations before going in the store and tries to ignore Lauren, her screaming will initially increase. It would be easy at this point for Mom to say to herself, "This ignoring doesn't work. I'm ignoring the behavior and it's just getting worse!" But it is imperative at this point that Mom continues to ignore this extinction burst. If Mom makes the mistake of responding to the burst, either by engaging with her, or by giving in and buying something for Lauren, she will be teaching Lauren that if a little screaming does not get her anything, **a lot** of screaming will!

> *When we ignore behavior, we must be prepared to survive the extinction burst!*

Surviving the extinction burst requires some tough love on your part. It is often difficult to ignore an inappropriate behavior, especially because you may be afraid of what others will think of your parenting skills. At those times, you want to focus on the long-term benefits for your children and have faith that this method will work. Your greatest priority is not to look like a good parent in the eyes of others, but to help your children mature.

> *If children hit during an extinction burst, remain calm and respond in a way that does not engage them.*

Because many parents have difficulty surviving the extinction burst, it is prudent to prepare for it in advance. Imagine what your child's extinction burst may look like. How will you respond? In most cases, it is best to go about your business calmly and pleasantly without any anger or show of frustration. What if your child responds to ignoring by grabbing or hitting you? You then want to use the least reactive means that will work with your particular child. You can calmly say, just once, "I need you to keep your hands to yourself," or "You may not hit. It hurts me when you hit." If your child stops hitting or grabbing, you want to give PVR for this, even if the screaming does not stop. If your child does not stop hitting, with no further words, you may calmly remove your child or yourself from the situation, perhaps to another room. If you are in a public place, you may want to go to your car temporarily or leave altogether.

One parent in our class shared a scenario that happened when she first tried the ignoring strategy. This mother had been having a difficult time when shopping with her four-year-old son, Ricky. Every time they went to the mall, Ricky would throw a tantrum until Mom would buy him whatever toy or object he wanted. Mom felt extremely frustrated and helpless in the face of her child's tantrums. She also felt very embarrassed when it happened in a public place.

After learning about ignoring paired with clear expectations, Mom tried this on their next trip to the mall. Before their arrival, she told Ricky that she was going to do the shopping and then buy him one small, specific toy. But when Ricky saw other toys he wanted, he started in on his tantrum to get a much larger and more expensive toy. Mom stated one time that the small toy was all she was willing to buy. Ricky significantly increased his crying, falling on the floor of the store and screaming. Mom picked him up and carried him to the car. He continued to scream throughout the walk through the mall and fought being buckled into his car seat. Although it was very hard, Mom did not engage with him verbally. To her great amazement, she shared that about two minutes into the ride home, Ricky stopped crying and became completely calm. At that point, she used PVR to praise him for calming down. This mom felt so empowered after this experience. She taught Ricky that despite his anger and loss of control, Mom would stay in control, remain steady, and keep him safe.

When parents successfully survive the extinction burst, without showing frustration, anger, or engaging ineffectively with their children, they often feel a sense of empowerment. They feel strong in the knowledge that they have not "given in" to negative behavior, and that they have modeled patience, resolve, and maturity for their children in the face of difficult circumstances. Keeping control of your emotions is the most challenging aspect of the *Keep It Positive* methodology and probably one of the most difficult skills to master. But the more you consciously practice this self-control, the easier it becomes, and the better your children will begin to behave.

In summary, these are the ideal steps when using ignoring as a tool to change behavior:

---

**Ignoring Inappropriate Behavior**

1. Set your **clear expectations and boundaries** before a particular event where you foresee a potentially challenging behavior.
2. Use frequent **PVR** to encourage any approximation to compliance.
3. **Ignore** any inappropriate behavior.
4. Be ready to survive **the extinction burst**.

---

Even when you have not had a chance to give clear expectations or boundaries, you may still use ignoring to respond to inappropriate behavior, but it is always more effective to set your clear expectations and boundaries before using ignoring as a tool.

Take a minute to list some behaviors you may have inadvertently reinforced that could trigger an extinction burst when you ignore them:

_____

_____

_____

## Use Limited Interactions for Health and Safety Issues

Sometimes ignoring is not an appropriate response to negative behavior. When the health or safety of an individual is at stake, you need to act in order to ensure that everyone is safe.

---

**When a behavior involves a Health or Safety Risk:**

- act to eliminate a dangerous situation with as little verbal interaction as possible,
- set clear boundaries,
- and positively verbally reinforce appropriate behavior.

---

Consider three-year-old Kyle, who throws toys at others. This clearly involves a safety risk to others. What should Mom do when Kyle throws? She should gently take Kyle away from the toys and from his friends and state matter-of-factly, "Kyle, I want you to play nicely with the toys and not throw them at your friends. You may play here by yourself for a while until you remember not to throw things." Mom uses this situation as an opportunity to teach, not to punish. She does this by setting clear boundaries for his expected behavior, and using a logical consequence of not being allowed to play with others if he throws toys at them. If Kyle starts playing appropriately by himself, she says, "Kyle, I like how you are making good choices when you are playing with your toys now." She continues to monitor the situation and looks for frequent opportunities (with a three-year-old, at least every two to three minutes) to give him Positive Verbal Reinforcement for playing peacefully. As he continues to play peacefully, Mom will be able to space out her PVR.

Suppose, after their initial discussion, Kyle tries throwing the toys at his friends again. Kyle already knows it's not acceptable to throw the toys at others because that clear boundary has already been set by Mom. Because Mom does not want to reinforce the behavior with negative attention, she should calmly pick Kyle up and say very briefly, "I am sorry that you cannot play with the toys now because you decided to throw them." Mom removes Kyle from the situation with as little verbal interaction as possible. Because of the risk of safety to others, ignoring alone is not an appropriate response to this behavior. But by calmly setting boundaries, reinforcing appropriate behavior, and having a logical consequence for inappropriate behavior, Mom teaches Kyle how to play peacefully with others.

Will Kyle learn this the first time Mom tries it? It will probably take a few times for the behavior to extinguish. After Mom teaches Kyle the lesson once, Kyle should now know that every time he throws things at someone, Mom will either take away the toy or take him away from the environment. Once a child has been taught, if the child hurts someone at an event that is enjoyable to him, it is often prudent to leave the event immediately. This may mean that you will have to sacrifice something you want to do, but the lesson your child learns will be worth your sacrifice. Stressing the importance of keeping others safe in this manner will usually have to be repeated only a few times before the behavior stops. Please note, though, that previously reinforced behavior will be harder to extinguish quickly.

Running into the street is another example of a behavior that obviously should not be ignored. What if two-year-old Brynne goes into the street? First, quickly and calmly, Dad physically removes Brynne from the street and says, "You may not go in the street without holding my hand. I would be sad if you got hurt." He places her on the sidewalk and says, "Play here instead." In this way, Dad sets his clear boundary and tells Brynne his clear expectation to hold his hand. Then he watches Brynne carefully and gives her PVR for staying on the sidewalk. "I like how you are staying on the sidewalk where it is safe." What if Brynne tries it again? Dad says nothing, and catches her before she steps off the sidewalk. He brings Brynne back to the sidewalk without a word. Dad only speaks to her to reinforce her positive behavior. If she repeatedly makes a run for the street, he might bring her inside, saying, "We're going inside now because I need you to stay out of the street." This is a logical consequence of Brynne's dangerous behavior.

A similar strategy would be used if Lauren, in the earlier example, were to start standing up in the shopping cart at the store, endangering herself. Mom would gently make sure she is seated and strapped, verbally give Lauren her clear boundaries, and make sure to frequently positively reinforce any approximation to staying seated. If Lauren continues to wiggle out of her seat, Mom would continue to act to ensure her safety, calmly with no anger, and with no verbal interaction. If Mom is not able to keep Lauren safe, she may leave the store and try again another time.

As you can see, behaviors that pose a health and safety risk are not to be ignored. But even in such cases, you want to interact as little as possible while eliminating the dangerous situation. You must take action to keep everyone safe, but you do not want your children's actions to become attention-seeking behavior. Remember that coupling your response with PVR makes your intervention much more effective.

Most inappropriate behavior does not pose a health or safety risk and can be easily addressed by ignoring it. List one of your child's behaviors that you would like to change by using ignoring as a strategy.

_____

_____

_____

What will you say to your child to set clear expectations and boundaries for this behavior?

_____

_____

_____

Now, imagine yourself surviving the extinction burst. Imagine what the burst will look like. How will you respond? Imagine yourself responding to the burst calmly, with complete composure.

_____

_____

_____

## Consequences: Two Types

Consequences can also be powerful behavior-shaping tools, as long as you are careful to not use them as punishment. As previously stated, punishment is not a long-term, effective way to change behavior. There are two types of consequences that can easily be used for positive reinforcement: consequences that are natural, and predetermined consequences that are related to the behavior.

## 1. Natural Consequences

Natural consequences are consequences that are not imposed by a parent, but that naturally and logically arise from a child's behavior. When used without any I-told-you-so's, or other forms of finger wagging or punishment, they can be extremely effective. The beauty of using a natural consequence is that it avoids a power struggle between the parent and child. The child's behavior simply causes an effect that stands by itself to teach the child not to repeat the behavior.

For example, nine-year-old Ben decides to have a breath-holding contest at school with his friend. Ben wins the contest by passing out and hitting his head on his desk. He wakes up in the principal's office with a cut on his head. Should Ben's parents punish him? No, because the natural consequence of passing out and hurting his head is most likely enough to deter such behavior in the future. If Ben's parents decide to punish him further, the lesson of the natural consequence may be diluted. The more attention given this kind of behavior, the more likely that Ben will repeat it.

In these types of situations, it is best to let the natural consequences speak for themselves.

In the passage that began this chapter, we noted that God "gives us what we want" even if it is bad for us. There is a natural and spiritual order to the world. This order contains the natural consequences of our actions. These consequences are designed to keep us on the path we need to follow. God does not ignore what we are lacking. God, as a perfect parent, desires that we seek Him out of love and grace rather than from fear. Which God would you rather follow; a God who vindictively punishes or a God who gracefully calls you home even when you make huge mistakes?

Consider, also, issues surrounding food. In our classes, numerous parents have asked for help with children who refuse to eat their meal, who are very "picky," or who take too long to eat. Parents often respond to these situations with statements like these: "You will sit at the table until you clean your plate," or "You must take a bite of everything." Although parents may feel they are encouraging their children to eat appropriately with these demands, they are actually creating a power struggle over food and exacerbating the problem. In our society, creating food issues with young children can often lead to serious problems later in life, such as anorexia or obesity. The fewer power struggles and obligations experienced around food, the better the chances are that your children will grow up with healthy attitudes about food.

Instead of forcing a child to eat, use natural consequences in situations involving food. What is a natural consequence of not eating? You feel hungry! A child who is hungry is more likely to eat. How does it work? Here's an example: Allison's daughter, Jenny, was a very picky eater. Allison had tried the "you must" approach, with no success. Then she tried the natural consequences approach. With this new strategy, when the family sat down to a shared meal, the food was served family style. The various options of healthy food were placed at the center of the table. Jenny could choose any of these options herself and add them to her empty plate, but Jenny chose to eat nothing. Jenny's parents did not remind, encourage, or verbally reprimand her about eating. When the meal was over, they calmly asked her if she was finished, and she said yes. Dad removed her plate and there was no further interaction over the issue. Jenny was not offered any other food or desserts.

This may seem like an outrageous plan to some parents. How can we just let our children not eat? Isn't it important to make sure they are eating healthy, appropriate foods? The truth is that missing a meal will not damage your child's health. Research shows that given an appropriate variety of healthy foods, children will generally choose a diet that meets their nutritional needs.[7] Young children will not starve themselves. For the most part, this only becomes an issue when children become teenagers and food becomes a powerful tool.

So what happened in Allison's household? For a few meals, Jenny continued to eat only what she wanted—a piece of bread, for example. Within three weeks, however, Jenny began to enjoy a variety of foods her parents would never have thought she would try—scrambled eggs, guacamole, and salmon, to name a few. As soon as Jenny's parents ended the family power struggle over food, Jenny began to feel empowered to choose new foods on her own, instead of feeling forced to eat them.

Another problem that was shared by most parents in our classes is "getting out the door on time with the children dressed and ready." The consequence of not getting ready in time may mean that your child will go to the event in her pajamas. This is not a punishment if it is done in a calm, nonaccusatory way. It is just a natural result of not getting dressed. When the time came for Sophie's mom to take her son Mitchell to school, Sophie was still in her pajamas, although she knew she was supposed to get dressed. Picking up Sophie gently, Mom calmly said, "It's time to go now," and she strapped her in the car seat. Sophie was flabbergasted that she was going out in her pajamas and began to cry, "But Mommy! I'm still in my pajamas!" Mom simply said with a calm and kind tone, "I'm sure that you will get dressed quickly next time." Sophie then suffered the embarrassment that was the consequence of her inaction. Mom only had to allow this to happen once for Sophie to learn to get dressed in time.

Remember Sara, in Chapter Three, who had trouble remembering to bring in her backpack? After positively teaching the specific expectation, Sara's mom did not remind her to bring it in any longer. Of course, even after this specific instruction, Sara would occasionally forget. What should Sara's mom do then? In the past, Sara's mom would get upset, ask Sara to bring in her backpack, and express frustration. Now, Sara's mom simply lets the natural consequence of leaving the backpack in the car to speak for itself. If Sara needs her backpack to do her homework, she will have to find it herself. Sara's mom expresses no frustration and simply continues to give PVR for any times that Sara remembers to bring in her things.

Most often, parents are reluctant to allow such natural consequences because of how they will appear to others. As a result of this reluctance, we have found parents who continue to dress or feed their children long past the age they can do it themselves. Out of desperation, one parent was even dressing her seven-year-old for him every day! But the desire to have others believe that your children are compliant or well-behaved is less important than giving your children the opportunity to experience the consequences of their own actions. We want to teach them to actually be responsible, not just look responsible in the eyes of others.

You can also allow natural consequences to occur regarding homework. Instead of punishing or verbally reprimanding your children about getting their homework done, you can allow your children to feel the natural consequence of embarrassment, a teacher-imposed consequence, or a bad grade on the assignment. This is very difficult for many parents to do because they often feel responsible for their child's homework. But whose responsibility is it really? When parents cajole, reprimand, and punish their children to complete homework, they take the responsibility out of their children's hands and put it in their own.

Parents can and should provide a structured time and place for their children to do homework. Parents can also help them with concepts or directions that they truly cannot figure out on their own. Parents should positively encourage and verbally reinforce their children's hard work, making it clear that they value education. But engaging in a power struggle over homework does not empower children to take responsibility for their own education, and, in fact, tends to encourage them to battle against it.

Many parents also feel responsible to make sure their children bring their homework to school, often making a special trip to take forgotten homework to school after class has already begun. This again does not allow children to take responsibility over their own homework and teaches them that it is the parents' job to ensure that it is submitted on time, not theirs. The sooner you empower your children to learn from their mistakes and handle their own age-appropriate tasks, the better prepared your children will be to face increasing responsibilities as they mature.

## 2. Predetermined Consequences

In place of natural consequences or ignoring, another tool that you can use is a predetermined consequence that is related to the behavior and stated in advance. Unlike a natural consequence, a predetermined consequence is imposed by the parent. To deal with repetitive problem behavior, before the behavior occurs, the parent states the expectation and the related consequence for not meeting the expectation. If the problem behavior does occur, the parent imposes the related consequence. Although this may sound much like a punishment, it is fundamentally different from a punishment in the ways shown in Table 5.

### Table 5
### Elements of Predetermined Consequences vs. Punishment

| Predetermined Consequence | Punishment |
| --- | --- |
| • Administered in a respectful, **non-punitive fashion**. | • Usually administered with the intent to punish, with a punitive tone. |
| • **Related** to the behavior. | • Often arbitrary — often not related to behavior, so child does not understand how punishment fits the misdeed. |
| • **Stated in advance** whenever possible. | • Often spur-of-the-moment decision, child has no warning of what will happen. |
| • Where applicable, **duration** of consequence is not an arbitrary length of time, but is **dependent on the child's subsequent behavior**. | • Duration is usually an arbitrary length of time — e.g., time-out for seven minutes, grounded for one week, no TV for three days. |

Wherever possible, it is best to state your consequences in advance and in a positive manner, only once. In subsequent situations where the same behavior may occur, your child should already know your expectations, and they do not need to be repeated unless your child is very young.

For predetermined consequences to work effectively, they must be administered in a way that is calm, respectful, and non-punitive. For example, sixteen-year-old Shelly is given the privilege of going out with her friends to a football game. Before she goes, her parents clearly state their expectations and consequences. "You may go to the game, but we expect you to come straight home afterwards. If you want to go anywhere else, please call and ask first. We are letting you go because we trust you and believe you are ready to make responsible decisions that demonstrate that trust." The implication here is that she will not be allowed out on her own if she breaches that trust.

Shelly returns home at the appointed time, but two days later, Dad finds out she was at a party instead of at the game. Shelly's parents calmly ask her where she was on that night, because Dad heard that someone saw her at a party. More than likely, Shelly will 'fess up. Shelly's parents express disappointment, but they do not lecture or rebuke her. "We're disappointed that you betrayed our trust, Shelly. You will have to earn it back before we feel comfortable letting you go out by yourself again."

The natural consequence of going to the party without permission is that trust has been broken. The predetermined consequence is that Shelly's parents will curtail her freedom to go out in the future. The next time Shelly asks to go out, her parents will show no anger or frustration, but state matter-of-factly that she may not go until she earns their trust again. Can Shelly regain her parents' trust? Absolutely, but she will have to earn that trust, which may be difficult.

> *The chief difference between a predetermined consequence and a punishment is in* **how** *it is administered.*

Although this result is parent-imposed, it is not a punishment because it is not administered in a punitive fashion. The chief difference between a predetermined consequence and a punishment is in **how** it is administered. Your tone of voice, the words you use, your facial expression and body language are all crucial elements that determine whether your reaction is a punishment or an effective use of a predetermined consequence. Remember to keep it positive.

What if Shelly's parents had said, "We can't believe that we trusted you and you lied to us! You are so irresponsible! When will you learn to be more responsible? You're grounded for a month, young lady!" The end result seems the same here. Shelly will not be allowed out alone for some time. But while the intent of the first scenario is to teach, the intent of the second scenario is to vent frustration and to punish. This subtle difference can be the determining factor in whether Shelly will feel motivated to truly change her behavior or act only out of fear of being caught and punished in the future. As discussed in Chapter One, punitive methods can also deteriorate the parent-child relationship, often encouraging secrecy, rebellion, or passive-aggressive behavior.

Because the goal of predetermined consequences is not to punish, but to change behavior, most consequences are not given an arbitrary time limit, but can be lifted once the child's behavior changes sufficiently for the better. As soon as Shelly demonstrates that she can behave responsibly enough to regain their trust, Shelly's parents will lift the consequence. How can Shelly regain her parents' trust? That would depend on the particular situation. If she shows genuine remorse, and goes beyond her typical level of responsibility, for instance with chores, homework, helpfulness, etc., Shelly's parents may feel that she is ready to try again.

The duration of the consequence is dependent on Shelly's change in behavior, which may take a week or several weeks. But in the punishment scenario, no matter how much Shelly changes for the better, she will be grounded until that arbitrary period of a month is over. Punishment offers no built-in incentive for Shelly to focus on changing her behavior. While punitive consequences encourage children to look back and focus on their negative behavior, effective use of predetermined consequences helps children look to the future and focus on change.

What would it look like if Jenny's parents used predetermined consequences in the situation involving her food issues? Before Jenny sits down to eat, Dad can say, "Mom made a good, healthy meal tonight that I think you will like, but if you decide not to eat it, we will not serve any other food." Dad is stating the consequence if Jenny rejects the meal — she will not be served any other food. He is also setting the parents' boundary regarding meals — they will not cater to a picky eater by preparing a separate meal. Making a separate meal reinforces the behavior of refusing to eat what is prepared. The resulting hunger that Jenny feels is the natural consequence of her choice. The refusal of the parents to make her an alternate meal is the predetermined consequence that is stated in advance.

> *Predetermined consequences must be*
> ***related*** *to the negative behavior.*

What kind of consequence is acceptable in the *Keep It Positive* method of parenting? Is it okay to ground a child for misbehavior? That depends on what problem behavior you are trying to discourage. It is important that the consequence be related in some way to the behavior. Jenny's parents did not respond to her pickiness toward food by sending her to her room. Instead, Jenny's parents said there would simply be no further food prepared for her. Lauren's mom did not tell Lauren that her whining and crying at the store made her lose her television privileges for the day. Instead, Lauren's mom simply took her out of the store and ignored her behavior. Trevor's dad, in Chapter Three, did not tell Trevor that his failure to get ready for bed on time would mean no playdates for the week. Instead, he made it clear that daw-dling would mean running out of time to read.

In Shelly's case, grounding was appropriate because she was disobeying the rules involving going out alone. But no-tice that the consequence was narrowly tailored to going out alone. She was not grounded from going out with her par-ents on family outings because there is no danger of Shelly betraying her parents' trust in that type of situation. The logic behind your consequence helps your child learn ex-actly what is being taught and lessens the potential for rebel-lion against arbitrary or excessive consequences.

When you are using predetermined consequences to manage behavior, it is important to state the consequence only once and then always implement that stated conse-quence when the inappropriate or difficult behavior occurs. Without the follow through of the stated consequence, the consequence holds no weight to change the behavior. Re-peatedly reminding the child of the predetermined conse-quence also takes the power away from the child to make the right decision.

Remember that with all consequences, the more matter of fact and calmly stated they are, the more effective they will be. This helps eliminate the power struggle because there is no one to fight against. As with ignoring, when you use pre-determined consequences that are stated in advance, you must be ready to survive any extinction burst that follows. Table 6 lists some examples of positive and negative ways that consequences can be administered. The negative im-plementation is illustrated to help your understanding of the importance of a calm and consistent implementation. The calmer you are when you administer the predetermined consequence, the less likely you are to invite defiance and rebellion.

**Table 6**
**Positive vs. Negative Administration of**
**Predetermined Consequences**

| Predetermined Consequences Stated in Advance | Positive Responses to Inappropriate Behavior ☺ | Negative Responses ∅ |
|---|---|---|
| We will play at the park if you stay where Mommy can see you. If you don't stay where I can see you, we will have to go home. | I'm sorry we have to leave, but I need you to stay with me so I can keep you safe. We'll try again another day. | If you don't stop running away from me, we're leaving! |
| I will answer your question when you ask politely. | *Ignore any whining or impolite requests.* | Can you just stop whining? I hate it when you whine and I'm going to ignore you when you do it. |

| | | |
|---|---|---|
| In our house, we take care of our responsibilities before we play. You can play your game after your homework is done. | Turn off the video game. You can play it after your homework is done. | You know you can't play your video game now. You haven't even started your homework. |
| You can play together if you can play nicely and work things out. | It seems like you two are having trouble working things out. You need to take a break from each other and play by yourselves for a bit in separate rooms. | Go to your room until you can stop fighting! You both have a time-out! |

Remember that you may avoid these situations altogether with:

- PVRs
- Clear Expectations before the possible behavior
- Structure
- Teaching not in the moment
- Ignoring

Natural consequences and predetermined consequences are powerful tools for positively shaping behavior. They often work well in situations where ignoring the behavior is difficult or inappropriate, such as in some cases of noncompliance, defiance, or when children are hurting each other.

Consequences are also sometimes preferable to ignoring if you are in danger of losing control of your own emotions. It is better to use a consequence than to get angry and become punitive after trying to ignore your child's behavior. As noted before, however, ignoring behavior and using PVR are generally more effective ways to extinguish unwanted behavior.

Take a few moments now to think of a few problem behaviors that you can minimize by using consequences.

_____

_____

_____

_____

_____

_____

What natural or related predetermined consequences would you use to help minimize those behaviors?

_____

_____

_____

_____

_____

_____

## Other Methods That Have Some Limited Effectiveness: Break Times

> *Time-outs are punitive and are not used in the*
> *Keep It Positive method. However, a nonpunitive*
> *break time can be employed.*

Are time-outs okay as a consequence? The *Keep It Positive* method does not encourage the use of time-outs as they are commonly used. They are usually administered in a punitive fashion, have an arbitrary time limit, and are almost always unrelated to the behavior being punished. There are some very limited times, however, when telling children to spend some time alone in another room is acceptable. Because our use of these break times is so different in both concept and application, we choose not to call them time-outs.

When children are fighting with each other, causing potential injury to others or to property, it is acceptable to say, "It seems like you two are having trouble playing nicely together. I need you to play by yourselves until you calm down and are ready to get along." Here, the consequence of not being able to play together safely is to play apart, in separate rooms if need be.

Notice that the consequence is not the child sitting on a chair to think about his bad behavior, nor banishment to his room, where he is allowed to do nothing but sit. These types of time-outs tend to fuel anger and resentment toward the parent and toward himself. Instead, the child is allowed to play by himself, just as long as he does it alone until he can play appropriately with others. Break times in the *Keep It Positive* method are administered calmly without being judgmental. Generally, when the child is ready to behave appropriately, he may try again.

## Tangible Reinforcement

Tangible reinforcement, which means rewarding desirable behavior with tangible things, can sometimes be useful, though it is generally the least effective method for changing behavior. Many parents are already familiar with this method because it is used frequently in group settings, especially in schools. A student may get a happy face stamp on his hand after a good day, a sticker for staying quiet and listening to the teacher, or a pizza party for turning in all homework assignments for the semester.

Though tangible reinforcement can sometimes be effective, it should only be used in support of other strategies, like PVR and consequences. If tangible reinforcement is used, it must be an immediate response in which the reward, or "reinforcer," is given directly after the desired behavior. The reward must also be phased out eventually, by shifting from consistent to random administration as behavior improves.

> **Tangible reinforcers are limited in effectiveness and are not a preferred method. To be effective:**
>
> - They should be used for a limited selection of **specific** behaviors.
> - Rewards must be given **immediately**.
> - Rewards must eventually be **phased out**.

An example of a limited, specific behavior where a tangible reinforcer can be effective is potty training. Some parenting books advocate giving a small candy treat for each appropriate step the child takes toward using the potty. This method can be used for potty training because it follows the principles outlined for effective use of tangible reinforcers. The reinforcer is used for a limited, specific behavior, in this case, using the potty. The treat is given out immediately after the child uses the toilet.

As success is achieved, the treats are slowly phased out. The child's growing pride often takes the place of the reinforcer. As Tommy starts using the potty more consistently, Mom can encourage independence from the tangible reinforcer by saying, "I like the way you ask to go to the potty before you need to go. You're really being responsible." Imagine if Mom did not fade the reinforcer. That would mean that as a grade school student, Tommy would still expect a treat every time he used the toilet. For the tangible reinforcer to work most effectively, it is also important to use PVR and do your best to give as little attention as possible to accidents or mistakes. Keeping your responses only positive and ignoring misbehavior will help motivate your child to focus on the achievement of the desired behavior.

Though usually ineffective, another popular use of the tangible reinforcer is a sticker chart for good behavior. Children receive stickers for good behavior, and after a certain number of stickers earned, the tangible reinforcer is given. The reinforcer given is often a toy or a special date with a parent. Although sticker charts are widely used, they are often ineffective in promoting long-term behavior change because the reinforcers are not immediate enough to be powerful. Most young children are not able to defer gratification for very long, and before the reinforcer is reached, the chart has often been forgotten. Even children who are motivated by sticker charts often start to lose enthusiasm for them over time as the novelty fades. Charts can also be time consuming and difficult to manage. It is far easier and more effective to give Positive Verbal Reinforcement for specific desired behaviors. PVR can be used just about anywhere at any time and its only cost is a few seconds of your time.

---

### Tangible Reinforcers are Less Effective because

- They are often difficult to implement.
- Their effectiveness tends to wear off as the novelty fades.
- They promote a "what's in it for me" mentality — your child may not internalize the positive values you are trying to encourage.

Tangible reinforcement has its place. It is most effective when dealing with a specific, limited, recurring behavior, such as using the toilet, staying near a parent while at the store, practicing piano, or remembering to put dishes into the sink. "Being good" is too general a behavior to use with tangible reinforcers. While the method may be useful in limited situations, it also has its drawbacks. When tangible reinforcers are used too often, children may develop a "what's in it for me" mentality and become more focused on rewards than on the satisfaction of behaving well. Instead, we want our children to internalize the values being taught, which is better facilitated by the use of positive teaching, PVRs, ignoring, and consequences.

## Choosing Your Tools

> *You will most often use a combination of tools to effect behavior change. Knowing what combination of tools to use and when to use them is not an exact science, but an art.*

In this chapter, we have presented the positive behavior support tools mostly in isolation for the sake of clarity. With most behaviors, however, you will probably use a combination of these tools. Knowing what combination of tools to use and when to use them is not an exact science, but an art. As you can see from our examples, the same behavior can be countered in different ways. For example, elements of nearly all the tools were present in the situation involving food issues. Jenny felt the natural consequence of hunger, the parent-imposed consequence of no further food, the ignoring that happened when she complained about not liking the food given, and PVR for trying new foods. Outside of the moment, not around mealtime, Jenny's parents can also positively teach Jenny the benefits of eating a balanced and diverse meal, and also teach polite manners surrounding her expression of feelings about the food served.

As the parent, you are always thinking about how to both teach and respond to behavior in effective ways, always tailoring your responses in logical ways to fit the situation. As you practice using these tools, you want to give productive thought to your own responses, evaluating what you are doing and what you can do differently. Your reflective parenting will make you increasingly skilled, and the positive interactions you have with your child will begin to come naturally.

The natural tendency of many parents who first learn the *Keep It Positive* method is to make consequences, tangible reinforcers, or punishment their default response and forget to use frequent PVR. As we have stressed many times throughout the text, the importance of PVR cannot be minimized. PVR should be your first tool when trying to change behavior. Even when using the tools in this chapter, you always want to couple them with PVR. When a child responds to ignoring or consequences by ceasing the negative behavior, you can say, "I like the way you are talking nicely now," or "Thank you for listening." When you see your child behaving appropriately at other times, you should continue to give PVR to those behaviors. Without PVR, the other tools will be far less effective.

## Chapter Four Summary

- Ignoring inappropriate behavior after clear expectations and boundaries
    - o is one of the best ways to eliminate behavior because any attention (positive or negative) increases behavior.
    - o means we must be prepared to survive the extinction burst.
- An Extinction Burst is the increase or escalation of an unwanted behavior before it becomes extinct.
- Natural Consequences are often enough to teach a child without further action from parents.
- Predetermined Consequences are implemented by the parent, but must be stated in advance and administered in a non-accusatory way in order to be effective.
- Positive Verbal Reinforcement is the most effective method of behavior change. PVR is essential to the success of the *Keep It Positive* method.

*Chapter Five*

.....................................

# UNDERSTANDING
# YOUR CHILD

## Hidden Messages and Communicating Feelings


*Do not let any unwholesome talk come out of your mouths, but only what is helpful for building others up according to their needs, that it may benefit those who listen. And do not grieve the Holy Spirit of God, with whom you were sealed for the day of redemption. Get rid of all bitterness, rage and anger, brawling and slander, along with every form of malice. Be kind and compassionate to one another, forgiving each other, just as in Christ, God forgave you.*

*— Ephesians 4:29, NASB*


The scriptural passage at the beginning of this chapter outlines the Apostle Paul's guidelines for our communication with each other. Take note of what Paul describes as "building others up" and "benefit[ting] those who listen." The power of positive communication cannot be overstated. We easily recognize the power hurtful words have. Often hurtful words are precursors of anger and even rage. Parents need to recognize that words are usually indicative of feelings. When faced with words of negativity, we have a choice to make. We can either ratchet up the negativity by becoming defensive or aggressive, or we can respond as Paul directs us to respond. Making the choice to build up our children when they are defiant or hurtful takes patience, self-control, mercy, and love. All of these are demonstrated to us by God. In the end, it is a matter of looking for the message behind the words. Thankfully, God looks behind our words and actions, to see the true nature of our hearts.

There is a powerful connection that both children and adults experience when they feel truly understood by a loved one. When you address the feelings underlying your children's behavior in a nonjudgmental way, not only do you help them manage their feelings and behavior, but you also connect with your children on a deep and intimate level. When you follow the practice of really listening to your children's hidden messages, your children will be more likely to trust and confide in you even through those challenging years of adolescence. By also learning to communicate your own feelings with your children effectively, you will engender their trust and nurture their capacity to feel empathy for others. This chapter will outline some simple ways to both listen to what your children are really saying and to communicate your own feelings in relationship- and empathy-building ways.

## Identifying Hidden Messages

All of us are influenced by our emotions. For example, when we are distressed emotionally, we may act with irritation and impatience with others. When we are sad, we may act with anger, as that is often simpler than showing our vulnerability. Children also experience the range of human emotions. But usually, their limited cognitive skills and development interfere with their ability to effectively manage these emotions. The *Keep It Positive* method offers some simple techniques to help you understand and respond to your children's emotions that may be driving their behavior. We refer to this process as determining the "hidden message" because children often do not have the tools to communicate what they are feeling.

---

## To Determine the Hidden Message:

1. Identify the basic emotions conveyed.

2. Acknowledge and empathize with the emotion.

3. Use good listening skills to enhance the above steps.

---

## 1.  Identify the Basic Emotions Conveyed.

When you are confronted with negative behavior, you want to remember that behavior is always communicative. One of the most important things that children are communicating through their behavior is how they are feeling. Because of their limited verbal and cognitive skills, children often cannot identify what they are feeling or why they are feeling it. Instead, they simply act on those feelings. As parents, you want to identify what that feeling is. You can then more effectively respond to the associated behavior. To simplify this process, we can categorize the multitude of human emotions into four basic ones: anger, sadness, happiness, and fear. Frustration can be seen as a type of anger, anxiety as a type of fear, loneliness as a type of sadness. For children, this can be simplified to "mad, sad, glad, or afraid."

To identify the underlying emotion, make an educated guess drawing from what you know about the way your child has reacted in the past, her personality, and the circumstances of the communication. For example, a child might poke and irritate her big brother because she is feeling lonely and she wants to play with him. She might respond rudely to a parental request because she is angry about an argument she had with her friends at school. She might bother her father while he is on the phone because she is angry that she has to wait so long for his attention. Or she might avoid studying for a test because she is afraid of failing. Discovering what your children are feeling will help you understand why they may be behaving in a particular manner.

Consider a situation involving hitting that a parent shared. Dad was in the elevator with his five-year-old daughter, Emily. After getting out of the elevator, Emily began to hit him. Dad believed that she was hitting him for no apparent reason, and said, "Stop hitting me!" with irritation. When we analyzed her behavior, however, we asked Dad what happened right before she began to hit. Dad said that she was upset that she didn't get to push the elevator button because Dad had unintentionally beaten her to it.

Mom, however, remembered that before Emily started to

hit, Dad had also said to a friend, "The things that kids get all wound up about. She's angry because she didn't get to push the button!" It wasn't until shortly after this that Emily began to hit. Dad did not realize that Emily's hidden message through her hitting was not so much "I'm angry that I didn't get to push the button," but "I'm angry that you talked about me and embarrassed me." By using her knowledge of her own child and by analyzing the situation at hand, Mom was able to understand the hidden message behind her daughter's anger.

## 2. Acknowledge and Empathize with the Emotion.

Next, you want to acknowledge and empathize with the emotion. Simply by acknowledging an emotion, you create a connection with your child that says, "I recognize what you are feeling and it is okay to feel that way." By sharing that you sometimes feel the same way in similar situations, you are empathizing with your child and letting her know that those feelings are natural and universal. When the child in the above example was bothering her father while he was talking on the phone, he could have responded by saying, "I'm thinking that you're a little mad that you had to wait so long for Daddy to talk to you. Sometimes, I get mad when I have to wait a long time too." Or, in Emily's case, "I think you are feeling angry because I embarrassed you in front of other people. I'm sorry that I did that. I know it's important to you that you get to push the button and I'm sorry that I made fun of it, but it is not okay to hit Daddy." While it is, of course, not acceptable for Emily to hit, Dad can acknowledge

Emily's feelings and empathize while still calmly setting a clear boundary about her inappropriate behavior.

> *Expressing empathy helps diffuse the intensity of your children's emotions, which helps them to move beyond them.*

Such expressions of empathy allow you to diffuse the intensity of the emotion, because your child feels the relief of being understood. Some of the overwhelming power of the emotion is abated, making it less likely that your child will act out those feelings in a negative way. Throughout this process, you want to use good listening skills to enhance all of the steps. We will discuss these skills a little later in this chapter.

Let's consider an example of how these steps may work with an older child. We use this illustration to demonstrate that these techniques are universal and can help anyone of any age. Learning the techniques while your children are young and then practicing them over the years can help to make communicating with your children much easier as they mature. Our example involves a parent who has practiced these skills since her child was young, so both parent and child have grown proficient at communicating with each other.

Jessica, the mom, was driving eighteen-year-old Tom to the dentist to have his wisdom teeth pulled. On the way, Tom was quiet and did not respond to his mother's attempts at communication, which was uncharacteristic for him. Instead of being irritated with his sullen mood, Jessica attempted to understand his hidden message. She said, "You are awfully quiet. Are you feeling a little scared about this procedure?" Tom admitted that he was fearful of the procedure and the pain that might result. Jessica responded, "I understand that. I am often afraid when I have dental work done too. Thanks for sharing with me that you are scared."

In this instance, Jessica followed the above steps. First, she realized that her son's communication (or lack thereof) was motivated by feelings and took an educated guess at what those feelings might be. Second, she verbally acknowledged his fear, and third, she empathized with it. Although Jessica could not fix her son's problem, she could empathize with him and allow him to share his fears.

Imagine if Jessica had said, "Don't be scared, silly. It will be okay!" Although that may appear to be comforting, it really isn't. It says, "I want to minimize your feelings and take away your fears." If she had said this, Jessica would not be empathizing with her son's feelings, but trying to fix them by commanding his fears away. How likely is it that Tom will share his fears in the future with either his parents or his future spouse? Not very likely. It is also unlikely that Tom will stop being scared just because he is told not to be. It is much healthier to know that it is okay to be scared about a possibly painful procedure and that someone cares about your fears. Parents cannot always fix everything for their children, and it is important to acknowledge that fact. We are not omnipotent, although our children may believe we are. The ability to express empathy without trying to fix the problem is a powerful way to convey that your children's feelings are important and that you care about them.

Our second example involves separation issues. One evening, Jill was leaving to come to our parenting class. Her seven-year-old son, Michael, started to whine and cry about her going. Jill tried to explain to him that she wanted to be a better parent for him by going to the class. Michael was still unhappy when she left. In class, Jill wanted to know if she did the right thing. We want to emphasize here that there is not always a right way to do something. Sometimes there is a better way, but that does not mean that what you have done is wrong.

We opened a discussion in class to determine the hidden message in Michael's communication to Jill. The message could be that Michael just did not want Jill to leave. He may have been trying to tell her, "I like it when you spend time with me at bedtime. I miss you when you're gone." Most likely, Michael did not care about why she was going; he still wanted her home with him at night. But Michael, being only seven, did not have the verbal or cognitive skills to express that. When we suggested to Jill that Michael might simply have been expressing his dismay at her absence, she agreed that was probably the problem.

So how can Jill address his feelings? Jill can respond to Michael by saying, "It seems like you are sad when I am gone at night and you really miss me. I am sad to leave you also and I miss you, too, when I'm gone." In this way, Jill can respond to Michael's hidden message of sadness. She empathizes with his feelings, but she does not try to fix them.

What if Michael continues to fuss after she has responded to his feelings? She should pleasantly kiss him good-bye, tell him she will see him in the morning, and leave without further interaction.

> *Our goal is to teach our children to learn to deal with disappointment, failure, sadness, and all of the other human emotions they will feel, without relying on us to fix everything for them.*

As parents, we often feel a need to fix every unhappiness that our children experience. This is not only impossible, it is unhealthy. Have you ever experienced a disappointment or a failure as an adult? Is it always fixable? Of course not. You want your children to learn to deal with disappointment, failure, sadness, and all of the other human emotions they will feel. If they rely on you to fix everything that happens, they will not develop their own skills to cope with the world. Your job as a parent is to help your children develop the internal skills that will support them in the outside world.

> *It is essential to allow children to have genuine emotions and to discuss them, because any feelings that are not expressed or addressed may return in unhealthy ways.*

In both of the above examples, it is not possible for the parent to fix the problem. Tom's mother could not help him escape the fear or the pain of dental surgery. Michael's mother cannot change the fact that Michael will be sad when she leaves for the evening. But in both examples, the parents can empathize with the problems and make it okay to talk about them. In the above situations, the idea is to give children (or young adults) the opportunity to share their feelings and for you to empathize with those feelings. In fact, it is essential to encourage your children to have genuine emotions and to discuss them, because any feelings that are not expressed or addressed can return in unhealthy ways.

When a parent becomes adept at empathizing with a child, the child's behavior changes for the better. Barbara, who had been in tears over her frustration with her twin boys during our class, later returned beaming with joy and excitement over the change that she had experienced. She had found the power of empathy with her children. She shared some of the new ways she responded to ongoing issues. "I bet it makes you feel so frustrated when you're trying so hard to clean up and your brother is dumping out the toys," and, "I'm thinking that you're feeling tired and want to take a little break from homework."

By learning to empathize with her children, she was able to see great changes in their behavior. They began listening more and throwing fewer tantrums. Her children had changed because she had changed herself. That change was her ability to understand their behavior and to view it in a different light. Once you begin to view behavior as serving a purpose for the child or communicating something important, you will tend to feel less frustrated and angry about challenging behavior. Instead, you can empathize with your children and allow them the opportunity to grow and mature at their own pace.

## 3. Use Good Listening Skills to Enhance the Above Steps.

Effective listening skills are essential to practicing all of the steps in discovering your children's hidden messages. Because these skills do not come naturally to most of us, they need to be practiced. When others talk, instead of focusing on what they are saying, most of us fall into the habit of focusing on what we want to say next. Sometimes we are distracted by other thoughts. Sometimes, instead of trying to see things from their point of view, we focus solely on how their message impacts us. Effective listening involves not only understanding the content of what is said, but also the feelings behind the message. How do we learn to be better listeners? We will offer four steps. It will be up to you to practice the steps.

---

### Effective Listening Skills

1. **Quiet** your mind when the other person is speaking.
2. Make **eye contact**.
3. **Reflect** to the speaker what you heard.
4. **Check** for accuracy.

---

First, quiet your mind when the other person is speaking. That means stop thinking about what you want to say next, the distractions of the day, or anything else going on in your mind. This is easier than it sounds, as you will find when practicing the technique. While the other person is speaking, make eye contact, which helps you to listen better. Then reflect to the speaker what you heard by paraphrasing what you think you heard the speaker say. Last, check for accuracy. Ask if what you heard is an accurate reflection of what the speaker was trying to convey.

Consider the following two scenarios involving four-year-old Emily and her mother.

### Scenario 1:

*Emily:*    Mommy, I love my new little pony play set! Don't you think it's SO cute?

*Mom:*    *(Mom is busy cooking and does not look up from her chopping.)* Uh-huh. Emily, make sure you put away all those pieces when you're done playing with them.

*Emily:*    Look it, Mommy! She's a rock star pony! *(Showing Mom a miniature pony with sunglasses on.)*

*Mom:*    Emily, I'm busy trying to get dinner ready, okay? Leave Mommy alone now.

### Scenario 2:

*Emily:* Mommy, I love my new little pony play set! Don't you think it's SO cute?

*Mom:* (*Looks up momentarily from her chopping and makes eye contact.*) Yes, Emily! It's really adorable. I'm so glad you enjoy playing with it.

*Emily:* Yeah! It's so fun! Look it, Mommy! She's a rock star pony! (*Showing Mom a miniature pony with sunglasses on.*)

*Mom:* That's funny, Emily, you made her look like a rock star! I like the way you are having fun on your own so nicely. That really helps Mommy finish cooking. You get to play with them a little more while I cook.

*Emily:* Okay, Mama.

In the second scenario, Mom followed the steps involved in effective listening. She stopped what she was doing, quieted her mind, made eye contact, and really listened. Then she reflected both the content and feelings of Emily's message by rephrasing them back to her to check for understanding. It is clear that both Mom and Emily understood each other and felt understood by each other in the second scenario. In this situation, Mom was able to continue her activity while effectively communicating with her daughter.

In the first scenario, however, it is not clear if either Mom or Emily heard what the other was saying. Emily's joy is lost on Mom, who inadvertently thwarts Emily's enthusiasm by telling her to clean up her toys. How might Emily feel in such a situation? She might feel confused or even angry that her mother is ignoring her.

How would we feel if we were in a similar situation? Imagine a situation involving John and Sue, a husband and wife.

### Scenario 1:

*John:*    The Yankees are in town this weekend. It's going to be a great ball game!

*Sue*:    Hmm-m-m-m? *(Does not look up from the paper she is reading.)*

*John*:    I said the Yankees are going to be in town and there's going to be a good game on Saturday.

*Sue*:    Uh-huh. Saturday, I was hoping we could go look at the new sofa I found.

## Scenario 2:

**John:**    The Yankees are in town this weekend. It's going to be a great game!

**Sue:**    *(Puts down her paper and makes eye contact with John.)* So the Yankees will be here? Sounds like you're excited to see the game!

**John:**    Yeah. I'm really looking forward to watching it on Saturday.

**Sue:**    Thanks for letting me know about the game. Maybe when it's over we can go look at that new sofa.

In this example, Sue did a number of things right. She stopped what she was doing and really listened to John. She reflected back what she thought she heard, and she checked for accuracy. Then she also validated John's feelings of excitement about the game. In which scenario is John more likely to want to join Sue to see the new sofa?

## Exercise V

To practice your listening skills, find a partner—a spouse, a friend, or a relative—and try this exercise.

**Partner A:** Speak to Partner B for 30 seconds, sharing one thing about your parenting that you have a concern about or that you feel good about. Give details.

**Partner B:** While Partner A is speaking, quiet your mind to hone your listening skills. After Partner A is finished speaking, reflect what you heard, validate feelings, and check for accuracy.

Next, switch roles.

When the exercise is over, reflect on your experience with each other and document it here.

_____

_____

_____

_____

_____

_____

_____

After you begin to practice these skills regularly, the ability to understand your child's hidden messages will flourish.

As with any new skill, it may feel awkward and difficult at first. The more you practice it in your interactions with others, the better you become. Soon you will find yourself learning more about your child and others through your effective listening.

Although you want to use good listening skills when you are able, there are, of course, times when you will not be able to listen to what your child is saying. You may be making a phone call, trying to concentrate on work, or in the middle of a conversation. At those times, you can use a variety of skills we have covered in previous chapters. Set your clear expectations for a particular event. "April, when I am on the phone, I want you to play by yourself so that I can hear what the caller is saying. Please wait until I am finished to talk to me." Give PVR for playing or waiting patiently while you are conversing. Ignore attempts to engage you, moving to another room if you have to. For young children, provide an engaging activity that they can do independently to make it easier for them to wait. If you need complete silence, it is best to schedule calls when your child is sleeping or not present, if possible.

One mom in our class also shared a technique she uses to help children find a break in a parent's conversation with others. This technique is useful because a parent's conversations can sometimes be quite lengthy, and it is often unreasonable to expect a child to wait for so long a period. To facilitate success, this mom taught her children to gently lay a hand on her arm to let her know they had something they'd like to communicate. She would then lay her hand on top of theirs to let them know that she was aware of their desire and would find a place in her conversation to stop and listen. This is a great way to respect children's communication while still teaching them to be polite.

## Effectively Communicating Your Own Feelings

Children are not the only ones who have feelings, of course. Parents do too. When you communicate your feelings to your children, you want to do it in a way that demonstrates how to effectively and respectfully communicate with others. By effectively sharing your feelings, you are helping your children to respond in a way that shows empathy and caring for others.

Consider a situation in which a school-age child speaks to you in a disrespectful way or talks back when you give an instruction. When it's an isolated incident, you may want to ignore the behavior. However, when the behavior is habitual, it is acceptable to teach the child how her behavior hurts you. But **how** and **when** you teach your child is as important as **what** you teach your child. With habitual behavior, right after the behavior, it is appropriate to say once (without anger), "I don't like it when you speak to me that way. It makes me feel sad and hurt." In this way, you set boundaries of behavior and help your child develop empathy for what you are feeling.

When expressing your negative feelings, it is best to say it only once, then ignore most other occasions where the behavior is repeated. Then, PVR whenever your child responds to you politely. When stated in a calm way, your expression of your feelings is not a punishment, but an appropriate response when someone does not treat you well. You are helping your child realize that what she does may be hurtful to someone else. This communication is much more effective than saying, "Stop talking to me like that! It is not nice!" — which is an angry reaction that targets the child as unkind. The first response identifies how you feel when the child speaks to you; the second targets the child personally. By modeling how to communicate your feelings, you can teach your children to appropriately communicate theirs.

One parent described her concern that her seven-year-old girl was becoming ungracious and "bratty." After receiving a free piece of candy from a merchant, she decided that she did not like the flavor and threw it to the ground. She had been exhibiting similar unseemly behavior on other occasions as well. Is all such behavior to be ignored? Or should something be said? As stated above, at times, when habitual behavior is occurring, it is important to address it. Again, how Mom addresses it here is crucial. "I'm disappointed that you threw the candy on the ground. It is important to be polite when someone gives you something no matter how you feel about it. Please pick up the candy and throw it away."

---

*When you express your disappointment instead of your anger about your children's behavior, you draw out their sense of remorse rather than their defensiveness.*

When calmly stated, this is very different from, "I can't believe you did that! What you just did was so rude! I want you to pick that up right now!" Even though the logical consequence of picking it up is the same in both responses, the first response shares Mom's feelings about the behavior, while the second sets Mom up for further defiance and confrontation. When you express your disappointment instead of your anger about your children's behavior, you draw out their sense of remorse rather than their defensiveness. It is important to limit the frequency of such expressions of disappointment, however, so that your reactions do not elicit attention-seeking behavior.

Eleven-year-old Tyler lived in a neighborhood filled with boys who enjoyed going to one another's houses and hanging out together. While this was okay with Tyler's mom, she also wanted to know where he was at all times. She asked him to call her each time he went to someone else's house, but Tyler was not very good about keeping this promise. Instead of lecturing, Tyler's mom shared her feelings with him. "Tyler, it seems like you've had a hard time following the rule about calling from where you are. When I am looking for you and I can't find you, I get really scared. I worry about what might have happened to you." Tyler did not want to make his mother worry, so he apologized. From then on, he was much better about remembering to call her. Helping children empathize with your feelings regarding a situation is often much more powerful than consequences or lectures.

While it is appropriate to express your negative feelings

on limited occasions in productive ways, it is also important to take the time to express your positive feelings toward your children as well. Affection, hugs, and high-fives are all important and wonderful physical ways to express those feelings. You express your happiness about your child's specific good behavior every time you give Positive Verbal Reinforcement. You can also express your pride in how much your child has grown in a particular area. "Ella, I am so happy that you are growing so mature. You are being such a good big sister. You've been sharing so well with Brianna and helping her when she needs it. I really appreciate that."

> *Expressly state your unconditional love.*

Above all, it is essential to make it clear that you love your children no matter what their behavior. That will never change. At a private time when you and your child are both feeling positive, with some distance of time from any misbehavior, you want to remind your child of this. "I love you so much. Do you know I love you even when you do something wrong? I sometimes don't like what you **do**, but I always love **you**, no matter what." If you are working on teaching patience, for example, you might also say something like, "It's hard to be patient sometimes, isn't it? It's hard for me to be patient sometimes too. We all have different things we can learn to do better, and the more we practice, the better we get. But you know, I will always forgive you when you make mistakes, and I know you will forgive me, too, when I make mistakes." In this way, your child will know that although your attention may only be obtained through appropriate behavior, your love is never conditional, but is always freely given. You are also modeling how to communicate positively with others.

## Unintended Hidden Messages and Labels from Parents

When faced with persistent negative behavior from their children, many parents begin to label their children "spoiled, selfish, sneaky, manipulative, mean, or disrespectful." It is understandable that parents who feel frustrated and challenged would begin to feel this way about their children. It is difficult to be met with challenging behavior on a regular basis. However, it is important to recognize how you are feeling and to realize that your perceptions will only increase their negative behavior. Even though you may never use those words with your children, your actions and tone can often convey your opinions.

Children are very good at sensing what their parents may be thinking about them, and they tend to meet negative expectations as well as positive ones. When children are thought of by others as selfish or dishonest, they may begin to unconsciously think of themselves as selfish or dishonest. Children then become stuck in the habitual behaviors that reflect those labels.

The good news is that when you move beyond that perspective and begin to see your children as capable of being something else, your positive vision can lead your children to see that vision also. Children will rise to your positive expectations when supported with positive parental teaching and guidance. When you begin to see them as kind or responsible, you give your children a tremendous gift—a confidence to believe in their own potential to be good.

A parent shared this story that exemplifies her confidence in her child's innate desire to be kind. Ten-year-old Scott was playing basketball outside. While shooting baskets, a mother of one of his friends playfully bumped him, accidentally spoiling his shot. Impulsively, Scott yelled, "Hey, stupid," at his friend's mother. Startled and angry, the neighbor left the area without saying a word. Shocked and upset by his mistake, Scott went into the house and sorrowfully shared this story with his mother.

Although she was disappointed, Mom did not get angry with Scott. After listening to his story, she could sense his true remorse. In response to Scott's mortified account, she said, "Scott, I'm sorry that you did that, and it sounds like you are really sorry for it too. Although I'm sure your words probably hurt Nancy's feelings, your sadness at your actions actually tells me what a good person you are. You wouldn't feel bad about what you did unless you were a good person. Thank you for telling me what happened. Can you think of something you can do to express to Nancy that you are sorry?" Scott then came up with a plan to write a letter of apology to the neighbor.

With this type of response, Scott's mom did not endorse his inappropriate reaction to Nancy, but helped Scott understand how to repair a relationship when he does something wrong. In addition, she helped Scott see what he did as an impulsive act and not a reflection of his character. While Scott's mom expressed her disappointment with the event, she also highlighted the good part of his nature, to help him see himself as someone who can respond to his own mistake in a kind and responsible fashion.

Scott's mom had practiced good communication with Scott for several years. This also allowed Scott to feel comfortable sharing his mistake with his mom instead of keeping it from her or waiting for the neighbor to convey the information. Like all of the skills in this chapter, practicing will add to your ability to utilize them effectively. Imagine if Scott had confessed this to his mom and she responded with anger and embarrassment over his behavior. Scott's ability to learn from his mistake and apply that learning to future situations would be significantly reduced. Instead, he might begin to believe that he is just a mean person and then exhibit that behavior. He would also be less likely to confess any other inappropriate actions or trust his mom to counsel him in the future.

You can move beyond your immediate negative reactions to similar problems by first taking the time to understand your children's behavior. Then, as their parent, you recognize that it is your responsibility to positively teach them how to respond in a more effective manner. Clear expectations, family values, Positive Verbal Reinforcement, teaching outside of the moment, and positively administered consequences are just some of the ways that we have discussed in previous chapters. Remember that children are not born mature. It is the parents' responsibility to teach them to become mature. When you continue to notice and recognize any approximation to positive behavior through PVR, and when you focus on your children's potential to become mature, your vision of them will begin to change, and so will your children's behavior.

A parent in one of our classes shared that she was afraid that her very intelligent eight-year-old was being mean to his friend Peter. When arguing with Peter, Mark's passion would sometimes lead him to speak harshly with his friend. Mom worried about Mark's ability to relate to others, and wanted to teach him to be gracious. Mom tried telling Mark that he was being "mean" and "arrogant," but he became defensive and defiant. The behavior continued because Mark started to see himself as habitually mean. Mark's mom had to stop labeling him and find a way to teach and encourage him to be gracious and humble.

One day, Mom listened while Mark challenged his friend Peter in a contentious debate. Mom stayed silent about it until the following morning. Then she said, "Mark, I really like the way you play and talk with your friend Jack. Whenever you disagree with Jack, you do it without getting upset. You often even laugh and smile while you argue about things. I would really like to see you do that with Peter too, because I know you care about others and want to treat everyone with respect."

Then Mom continued, "You know, you and I are a lot alike. Sometimes I feel strongly about something I believe too, and I get a little too passionate when I talk about it. I've made that mistake with one of my friends in the past, and soon I could see that she was starting to avoid talking to me because she didn't feel safe. That made me feel really bad, and I apologized to her. I learned from my mistake that I need to always consider other people's feelings even though I might think I am right. I learned that I have to be careful how I say things to others." Mom's openness and nonjudgmental attitude toward Mark resulted in further discussion from him and culminated in a hug and an "I love you, Mommy" from Mark!

Children want to be supported out of their habitual negative behavior. But like all of us, they do not want to be judged. When parents can teach in a way that invites relationship-building, problem-solving, and understanding, they reap the rewards in a relationship that is based on mutual respect and trust, as well as in changed behavior. The interaction that Mark had with his mom was only possible because Mom had been using positive behavior support techniques for many months. Because Mark was beginning to trust her more, Mom was able to teach in a positive way — affirming Mark's interactions with his other friends, sharing her expectations for his behavior, and sharing her own personal story.

Sharing personal stories of your own struggles or lessons learned is a great way to build bonds of mutual trust and respect. Mark knows that he is not unchangeably "mean," because his own mom had admitted to making the same human mistake. Mom has also told Mark, "I know it's hard to talk nicely to your friends sometimes. I have noticed that you have really worked hard to improve that, and I know you will continue to because you are a kind boy." Mark knows that his mom will always believe in his innate ability to be kind. He further knows that she will encourage and support him as he practices kind behavior, and she will forgive him for mistakes that he may make along the way.

## Addressing Untruthfulness

One form of a hidden message is apparent when children are untruthful. When children are untruthful about a particular behavior, their hidden message is really, "I'm scared because I did the wrong thing and I do not want to be punished." Understanding this hidden message and empathizing with it is an important part of guiding your child to tell the truth even when it is difficult or scary. "I know it's sometimes hard to admit when you've done something wrong, but by telling me the truth we can work it out together." It is important for children to know that although you may be disappointed with their behavior, you will be proud of them for taking responsibility and not compounding the problem by lying.

Understandably, a parent's initial response to untruthfulness is often to get angry. Most parents are appalled when their children "lie" to them, fearing that this behavior may be indicative of a moral failing in their children. In an attempt to nip it in the bud, parents often confront their children by angrily asking, "Why did you lie to me?" While the answer is obvious, children do not have the cognitive ability to express the true reason, which is usually to avoid their parents' anger, disappointment, or punishment. This question only backs the child into a corner and serves no purpose.

> *Do not ask your children questions that make it easy for them to lie. Express your disappointment, but recognize that telling the truth can be difficult. Parental anger about lying drives children to lie more, not less.*

Parents also often ask questions like, "Did you hit your brother?" or "Did you draw on the wall?" The parent already knows the answer, but wants the child to admit it. But asking such questions gives young children more temptation to lie than they can usually bear, especially if they are often punished for such behaviors. It is better just to say, without anger, "I am thinking that you drew on the wall, and I am disappointed because you know our rule. Please help clean it up." By laying all your cards on the table, you address the issue without putting your child through a test that sets them up for failure.

Notice that the child is not "off the hook," and must still have the logical consequence of cleaning it up, but the child is not told to do so in a punitive manner. When the child does help, Dad can say, "Thank you for helping. You took responsibility for what you did, and I like that." By giving PVR for any approximation to taking responsibility, you encourage children to take responsibility more often.

Many parents also try the lecturing route, hoping that by

shaming the child, the child will never lie again. "I can't believe you lied to me! It's really wrong to do that. Don't you know that God doesn't want you to lie? Do you want people to call you a liar?" But by lecturing in a punitive way, the child will start to think of herself as a liar, and she will probably live up to that expectation.

Instead of lecturing, you can have a discussion with your child about the importance of truthfulness in a constructive manner, but again, not right after the lie takes place. At a different, more peaceful time, discuss with your child the natural consequence of being untruthful, which is a loss of trust. Discuss what might happen when you lose someone's trust. The story of *The Boy Who Cried Wolf* is a great way to begin this discussion with younger children. As shown through numerous other examples throughout our text, our goal is always to teach in a positive, rather than in a judgmental or punitive manner. This is not only a kind way to parent, but also a way that works most effectively. Giving PVR to any situation where your child is truthful against her own self-interest is also a wonderful way to teach truthfulness.

## Unintended Labeling in Sibling Rivalry

Parents often run into the problem of sending unintended hidden messages in dealing with sibling rivalry. While a dispute might be set off by any number of issues, at its core, persistent sibling rivalry is almost always about the parents. Parents are often confused by this statement. They sometimes think, "How can it be about me? It's because his sister is always so mean to him. It has nothing to do with me." Although his sister's action toward him may be the reason why Tim yelled at his sister, when parents look beyond the surface, they can see that his behavior is often motivated by an underlying desire.

That desire is most often related to the parents. Sometimes children simply want to draw parents into the situation because they want the attention. Parents often make the mistake of taking the bait by trying to figure out who started it, who was at fault, and how to fix the situation. The hidden message that parents send is "I don't think that you can solve this problem on your own. I need to get involved and fix it for you." This attention that children get from their parents for arguing then increases the bickering, because as stated in Chapter Two, attention increases behavior. The less you intervene in conflicts and the more you encourage your children to solve their own problems, the less sibling rivalry will occur.

> *Avoid labeling your children as "the instigator"*
> *or "the victim" in any given conflict.*

Aside from increasing conflict, the most damaging problem with intervening is the danger of labeling your children in negative ways as discussed in the previous section. In the case of sibling rivalry, when you reprimand one child, your hidden message is that the child is "the troublemaker, the instigator, the mean one," while the other becomes "the victim," which can be equally damaging. Even though you are not consciously thinking of your child in this way, your actions of reprimanding and saving make those messages clear to your child. Many parents have shared that they have begun to actually see their children this way, and they use various labels to describe them.

What **can** you do to decrease sibling rivalry? First, realize that a certain amount of conflict is normal sibling behavior. By understanding that some conflict is normal and typical, you will be less likely to be reactive in response. Then, use the methods described in previous chapters to decrease the excess conflict that may be occurring in your household. Make sure your children understand that your family values are to love one another and treat each other with respect. It is also important to model with others (spouses and children) how to effectively communicate during a conflict. Children do as we do, not as we say.

Specifically teach them to "use their words" with each other, to talk to each other in productive ways instead of running to a parent to solve their problems. When children are young and verbally fighting, for example, you may want to give them alternate words to use when communicating their thoughts. Instead of "I want that, this is mine!" you may teach them to say instead, "I want to play with that, can I have it back please?" The skills involved in good communication and problem solving (listening, walking away from a conflict, cooling down, compromise, negotiations) are all teachable skills that can be taught outside of the moment of the conflict. Role playing and discussions are useful during this time. Teaching them at the moment of the conflict is usually not effective. The heightened emotions of the moment will cause your lesson to fall on unreceptive ears.

When you know they have the skills to resolve their issues, say, "I'm sure you two can figure out a way to solve your problem," and do not intervene unless there is a health or safety risk. When conflicts become too intense, you may calmly say, "It seems like you two need to take a break from each other. I want you to play by yourselves for a while until you're ready to play together again." Separating them into different rooms in a nonpunitive way may also be necessary to prevent further interaction and provide a time where they can cool down.

Most importantly, you want to encourage them with PVR whenever you see any approximations to getting along with each other. "I like the way you used your words to tell him to stop touching you." "That was great how you walked away from her when she didn't stop hitting. That took a lot of self-control." "I like how you were able to work things out with each other. That was good compromising." Always be on the lookout for any positive interactions. "I like the way you two are playing together so nicely. It seems like you're having a lot of fun with each other." "That was nice of you to help your sister with her shoes." "Thank you for picking that up for your brother." Doing this very frequently at first will begin to result in a more peaceful sibling relationship, and then you will be able to gradually lessen your PVR.

You can also decrease sibling rivalry by calling attention to the benefits of fostering a caring relationship. "I like how you two are having so much fun together. You know, friends will come and go, but brothers are really special. You will always have each other, and as you grow older, you'll always be there for each other." They will learn to see your vision of what a positive sibling relationship can look like.

Sibling rivalry also occurs when one child feels she receives less attention or love than the other. There are many reasons why one child might feel inferior to another. Different natural gifts, birth order, different levels of good behavior, even different genders may garner different levels of attention in a child's life.

It is important to be mindful of what your children might be feeling about their roles in the family and how you may be unintentionally validating those feelings. On a regular basis, take the opportunity to express your love and appreciation for each individual child for being the unique individual he or she is. Your child's increased sense of security in your love will make a huge impact on the way your child interacts with his "competition." When children feel truly loved and accepted, they will be much less likely to feel the need to compete or to take their underlying anxiety out on their siblings.

### Exercise VI

Try to find the hidden message in one of your child's communications and then use the skills that you have learned to acknowledge and empathize with his or her feelings. Write down what your child said and how you responded.

_____

_____

_____

_____

_____

_____

_____

## Chapter Five Summary

- Children do not always communicate effectively or even know exactly what they mean to communicate.
- When you discover the hidden messages in a child's behavior or speech, you can empathize with your child and better formulate a more appropriate and effective response.
- Use good listening skills by quieting your mind, making eye contact, and reflecting back what is said, to foster strong trust and caring with your child.
- Share your own feelings with your children to help develop their character and empathy.
- Be careful not to label children. Change your vision to see them at their highest potential.
- Understand the hidden message behind your children's untruthfulness and do not ask them questions that make it easy for them to lie. Express your disappointment, but recognize that telling the truth can be difficult.
- Sibling rivalry is almost always about the parents.

The power of a parent should not be underestimated. Teach outside of the moment, without intervening in conflicts.

- Expressly state your unconditional love. Make sure you let your children know that you will always love them no matter what.

*Chapter Six*

....................................

# PUTTING IT ALL TOGETHER
## Internalizing Behavior and
## Tips for Staying Positive

*Love is patient, love is kind and is not jealous; love does not brag
and is not arrogant, does not act unbecomingly; it does not seek
its own, is not provoked, does not take into account a wrong
suffered, does not rejoice in unrighteousness, but rejoices with
the truth; bears all things, believes all things, hopes all things,
endures all things. Love never fails...*

*— 1 Corinthians 13:4-8a, NASB*

The *Keep It Positive* methodology is a new approach to parenting because it emphasizes the changes that you, as a parent, will make to successfully implement these principles. In the beginning of this journey, you may have been skeptical, wondering if positive behavior support could work for you and your child. We hope that by now you have already begun to experience success with the program at home. This chapter will help to summarize all of the facets of *Keep It Positive,* along with recommending a variety of ways to support you as your children grow and mature. Although the *Keep It Positive* methodology will not eliminate all inappropriate behavior, it does provide you with a blueprint and guide to successfully manage behavior and to apply the principles to new situations that will surely develop.

Full implementation of the *Keep It Positive* methodology requires a dramatic shift in your attitude, your behavior, and your point of view. This change begins with understanding that all behavior is purposeful. Children's behavior is designed to communicate something, to gain access to something, to escape some activity, or just to get attention. You learned that any behavior that receives either positive or negative attention will increase.

The first step in implementing the method is to develop family values that address the internal skills you want your children to learn. Then specifically teach those values to your children. It is also important to teach clear, positive expectations for specific behaviors. Children cannot meet your expectations for good behavior unless you have clearly communicated those expectations to them. Provide structure and boundaries to facilitate success while always considering the age and developmental level of your children.

We have also discussed the many tools you have to help teach your children discipline. Those tools are ignoring, consequences (either natural or predetermined and related to the behavior), and best of all, positive verbal reinforcement (PVR). Teaching your children self-discipline is very different from punishing them. Although punishment may work immediately for an inappropriate behavior, it does not effect long-term behavior change. We hope you have discovered that long-term internal change in your children is much better than the short-term effects of punishment.

One of the most valuable facets of *Keep It Positive* is to listen carefully to what your children say and to value their dignity and self-worth. We have discussed the importance of addressing your children with the same kindness and grace that you would want them to offer to you and others. If you offer this gift to your children, we guarantee that you will reap the long-term rewards of this gift.

For example, you may observe your child offering kindness and dignity to others as they mature. One parent who implemented the *Keep It Positive* method for many years shared a story about her twenty-one-year-old-son, John, and his great display of kindness and love to his ninety-two-year-old grandmother. Although he was currently away at college, even during a short visit home, he did not fail to budget time to spend with his grandmother, who lived another hour away. He visited her, took her places, and spent time with her without any prompting from his parents. Although young adults of this age usually have the priority of spending leisure time with friends, John had learned his family value of kindness and support to others through his parents' teaching and modeling. John now demonstrates that he has internalized this value. As a parent, this is when you know that your child will live out the values you cherish for the rest of his life.

Accepting and implementing the principles of *Keep It Positive* is to imitate how God has parented us. Consider the words of scripture about love in light of the old habits you may have formed as a parent and are now beginning to break. First and foremost, remember that even when you have made mistakes in parenting, you have made them out of love, not malice. We hope that from this book you have discovered a way to parent your children that reflects the love you have for them. We hope you have learned to "not be provoked" and to let go of the "wrongs done to you."

Love is at the very heart of parenting. Your mission as a parent is to teach your children not only certain life skills, but also certain love skills. If you can succeed at helping your children to love and to be loved, you will have changed not only your children, but in a sense, the whole world. *Keep It Positive* is about parenting with integrity. When you parent with positive affirmation and structure, you convey the deep sense of love you have for your children. Isn't this how God parents us?

## Internalizing Values and Generalizing Behavior

Is there a point where it is no longer necessary to positively reinforce everything a child does? The short answer is "Yes!" The goal of positive behavior support is not to raise children who are dependent on your positive attention to behave well. Instead, it is to help children internalize self-control and values so that they make good decisions and behave appropriately in most situations.

## Helping Your Children Internalize Values

1. Believe in your children's innate desire to do well, and communicate that through praise and love.
2. Begin to taper down PVR as a child masters a particular skill.
3. Encourage children to focus on how the successful behavior helps them feel the internal pride of accomplishment.

How do you help your children internalize the values you want them to learn? First, integral to positive behavior support is your belief that your children can and will behave appropriately. When parents have faith in their children's ability to behave well, children also begin to have faith in themselves. When a parent notices and regularly points out good behavior, children begin to see themselves as being kind, responsible, and capable of making good choices. After using PVR regularly and cultivating relationships based on trust, communication, respect, and love, you will see that children will often behave appropriately even when they are not being "noticed" by anyone.

Second, as you begin to observe positive changes in your child, you can start to reduce the frequency of PVR. When your child takes responsibility for "getting out the door on time" on a regular basis, or when the homework wars have quieted down significantly, you can give PVR less often for those particular behaviors. This does not mean that you stop recognizing the good in your child. It is still important to sometimes remind your children of all they have accomplished. "I've been noticing how you are responsible for getting to school on time each day. I bet you feel pretty good about that." By focusing on how this success makes your child feel, you are encouraging him to value his work and accomplishment as its own reward, and not just for your praise.

Internalization of skills also leads to generalization of skills. When your children become responsible in one area, that accomplishment can spill over into other areas, because they have experienced the internal reward of a job well done. Generalization is the goal. Using the skills you learn as a positive parent will help direct your children to internalize their own values and accomplishments and then help them apply those values to other areas of their life.

Remember, however, this does not mean that they will never make choices that disappoint you. They are human, after all, and make mistakes just as you do. But when you have fostered a relationship of openness and respect through your listening and supporting skills, it is much less likely that your children's poor choices will be ones that carry significant risks.

## Dealing with Negative Influences

Once you begin to implement the *Keep It Positive* methodology in your home, you will become aware that many structures in our society do not practice this type of interaction with children. You may begin to notice that some of your children's teachers or coaches can be very punitive. This can be especially troubling when you have worked hard to eliminate negativity at home. You may feel disturbed to learn how your children are exposed to negativity in other settings.

Know that you cannot change those outside situations. We do encourage you to try to find coaches and others who encourage children, rather than ones who are critical and punitive. But because those involved in sports activities are often volunteers, your ability to control these situations can be very limited. Although such a realization can be troublesome, the nature of your children's character will be based mostly upon their interactions with you. You can lessen the impact of such situations by giving your children your own positive feedback after an event. Saying things like, "I like how hard you worked to catch the ball on the field," or "You are learning lots of new dance steps in your class. You are really working hard and I think you are having fun also," is a way to encourage and support your child.

Leave the corrections and teaching to the coaches and instructors rather than adding that to your parenting responsibilities. Many parents can become very invested in a child's performance in sports and other extracurricular activities. Remind yourself that such activities are for your child's enrichment and not generally for a future career. The percentage of boys who play Little League baseball and actually go on to the major leagues is miniscule. If you approach a sport or dance activity as a wonderful opportunity for your child to learn team participation, have fun, and develop friendships, and not as an audition for a future career, you can help them to enjoy such activities and help them keep things in perspective. Arm your children with your love and your appreciation for their character, and most of that outside negativity will not affect them.

## Parental Unity

Consistency between the parents is a critical component to the success of the *Keep It Positive* method. As you can probably imagine, if one parent is using PVR and one parent is being critical and negative, that negativity will overshadow the positive interactions. Similarly, if one parent is using ignoring and logical consequences to address inappropriate behavior and another is punishing or indulging the child, the effectiveness of this methodology will be significantly reduced.

Often, in our classes, our parents say that it helps to have both spouses attend the classes together. This allows them to collaborate on the implementation, providing consistency for their children. Likewise, we encourage you to share this book with your spouse, a noncustodial parent, grandparents, or any other regular caretakers your children may have.

Communication between partners is an important piece so that all caretakers are in agreement and working together. We encourage you to discuss the aspects of positive behavior support with your spouse or others to support each other in the implementation. But just as you do not want to point out your child's mistakes, it is important not to point out when you feel your spouse is doing or saying the "wrong" thing during an interaction, and especially not in front of the children. Wait until later in the day, when emotions are less intense, and when you have given some thought about how to approach the situation diplomatically. Understand that it is a difficult thing to change old habits, and give the same grace to your partner that you would want given to you.

## Ways to Facilitate Self-Change

By now you must realize that changing yourself is both the most difficult and the most important part of this process. Changing established habits is not easy, so we offer the following tips to help facilitate this change.

## Take care of yourself.

Any new skill is much more difficult when you are tired or stressed. Get enough sleep, practice healthy habits, and foster supportive relationships that help sustain you.

## Allow yourself time to analyze a behavior.

It is not always easy to apply positive principles in the midst of an inappropriate behavior. If you are in the middle of something where you are not sure how to react, and you are beginning to feel like screaming and punishing, take a step back. In most cases, it is okay to wait to react. When you are calm, try to consider the purpose of that behavior. Give yourself a little time to think about it and decide upon your next best action for the situation. This may also allow you to "ignore" something inappropriate at that time. Usually the behaviors that cause you the most stress and frustration are the ones that will take the most work for you to change your responses to. It is important to approach the process in a thoughtful way.

## Be reflective after an interaction.

Review your previous interactions and see if you could have acted more effectively in a particular situation. Most situations come up repeatedly, so reflecting on your previous actions and having a plan in place for next time will lead to future success. The most reflective parents are often the most successful parents.

## Plan ahead.

Most problem behaviors are recurring. Plan out your course of action for a particular problem behavior so you will be ready to respond in a positive way.

## Catch your child being good.

PVR is not simply about trying to change an inappropriate behavior. It is also about recognizing and valuing those wonderful character traits in your child. When you observe these, **speak up.** Let them know how much you appreciate their helpfulness, kindness, and other family values. This will also get you into the habit of using PVR in a natural and consistent fashion. Some parents initially wear a rubber band around their wrist or have some other symbolic reminder, like a sticker or sticky notes, to remind them to look for opportunities to be positive.

## Focus your targets.

Trying to change everything at once is overwhelming for both you and your child. Focus on one or two behaviors at a time to facilitate success. Also, pick your battles. Recognize that your children are still children, and focus on instilling the values that matter most to you.

## Create regular opportunities for positive interaction.

Sometimes we spend so much time responding to behavior, implementing schedules, and getting our children into group activities, we fail to provide the simple family interactions that everyone enjoys. One of the blessings of having young children is that you get a chance to be childlike again. Enjoy a family walk or play a family game together. Use dinnertime to share stories about your day rather than working on manners. Children will remember and value these opportunities to interact with you much more than dance classes, sports, and scouting. Although lessons and clubs are wonderful things to offer your children, do not cram your schedules so full that you miss the fun of just being a family together.

## Remember to let your children know how much they are loved.

Give them lots of kisses and hugs, special stories at bedtime, a listening ear, and anything that communicates how important they are to you.

## Seek support.

As we suggested in Chapter One, *Keep It Positive* is not a quick fix or an easy solution to your children's inappropriate behavior. It takes time, patience, and practice to implement effectively. Because it is often difficult to implement new habits, we encourage you to join or begin a *Keep It Positive* support group. This is where parents who have taken our classes or read this book meet together with a facilitator on a monthly basis to support one another. Make it a habit to attend and be refreshed on the method. You may also want to read this book with friends and relatives and open dialogues with them to discuss how things are going. Parents supporting parents is a powerful way to ensure that you can continue to provide your children with loving, positive support as they grow and inevitably bring you new challenges. For more information, go to www.keepitpositive.net.

As we conclude our guide to the *Keep It Positive* method, we want to remind you of several key points. All of the parameters of the method must be implemented and tailored to your particular child. We encourage you to embrace your child's individuality and to value and uphold the essence of his or her character. Although this book has offered many examples of what to say or how to say it, we encourage you to develop your own style and use your own words. The important principle of positive interactions is not about the specific words you say, but more about how you communicate.

As you become more comfortable with PVRs, they will come more naturally to you and will be a part of your general communication pattern with your children and with others. This is the goal. In the beginning, you want to think about what you say, but as you practice, it will become easier. You will begin to notice the positive actions in your child before you notice the negative. Celebrate this! It means that you have embraced the philosophy and you are a model for your child.

Be careful, though, as it is easy to fall back into punitive and negative interactions. The *Keep It Positive* method takes practice and dedication to implement effectively. Because this methodology goes "against the grain" of conventional wisdom, it is easy to fall back into old ways. At the end of this book, we have included a few charts to help you see the entire method at a glance. The chart entitled "Putting It All Together" can serve as an easy reference to remind you of all the elements and strategies of the *Keep It Positive* method.

Above all, remember that *Keep It Positive* is a wonderful gift to yourself and your family. Our hope is that as you embrace this process, you will allow yourself to learn and grow as you practice it. We also hope that you do not expect to be perfect. As you begin to encourage and forgive your children for their mistakes, you will also forgive yourself if you make some of your own. You will allow yourself the time to learn and grow in this new way of parenting and will then model these attributes to your children. If practiced consistently and purposefully, *Keep It Positive* can bring harmony and peace to your home in a way that you have not imagined. You can make it happen!

## Review

Here is a simple review to help you understand how much you have learned. Go back to the first chapter and pick one of the most challenging behaviors that you wrote down. Think about that behavior and write about how it is different now than it was when you first considered it.

_____

_____

_____

_____

_____

_____

_____

What are you particularly proud of doing in a particular interaction with your child or children?

_____

_____

_____

_____

_____

_____

_____

How has this methodology positively impacted your home?

_____

_____

_____

_____

_____

_____

_____

Consider one or two ways that you believe your children have begun to internalize the skills you want them to develop.

_____

_____

_____

_____

_____

_____

As you have begun to realize, the *Keep It Positive* method is successful because it is simply the way that all people would like to be treated. All people — children, spouses, employees, friends, and relatives alike — want to be treated with respect, encouraged with kindness, spoken to with honesty, and accepted for who they are. *Keep It Positive* is not a trick, nor is it simply a methodology. It is a way of being and interacting with others in ways that are caring, encouraging, and supportive. It is about building relationships that are based on trust, honesty, empathy, and love.

When your children's behavior begins to improve, understand that the changes you see are because **you** are changing. You are beginning to see your children in a new and different way—in a way that communicates that they are wonderfully made. This is the same way that God views us. God loves us and accepts us unconditionally, offering us grace and forgiveness when we err. This is the gift that positive behavior support can offer your children—the gift of knowing that they are loved and valued, that you have faith in their ability to do good, and that you will teach them how to live, learn, and grow to be a positive force in the world.

..................................................

## Chapter Seven

# KEEP IT POSITIVE FOR CHILDREN WITH SPECIAL NEEDS

## *Tailoring the Fit*

Parents of children with special needs are often discouraged when it comes to finding advice and support for their parenting skills. The majority of the literature on this subject is academic in nature and not readily accessible to the average reader. The good news is that *Keep It Positive* is a methodology based upon research and implementation of these practices on students with significant behavioral difficulties and disabilities. The process of positive behavior support was developed in schools and residential settings that work with children with disabilities. The disabilities in these settings varied from mild Attention Deficit Disorder, to more significant Autism Spectrum Disorders and other developmental disabilities.

It was frequently noted that such students had increasing behavior problems along with their disabilities. The knowledge that children's behavior is always purposeful and communicative was learned through observation and data collection with this population. Interventions such as ignoring, logical consequences, and other methods were implemented with documented success. The *Keep It Positive*

method was based upon the demonstrated reduction in behavior problems seen with these children. Juda Carter has
worked closely with many children with disabilities and has
implemented and observed these improvements in her career.

For children in our society who have difficulty learning
and communicating, behavior is often the only means of
getting their needs met. For years, practitioners tried to
change their behavior through punishment and restriction,
with the most severe problems resulting in institutional
placement. The development of positive behavior support
was the key to helping students with disabilities learn to
function in society. As you apply this skill to your parenting, you can practice what researchers have learned is the
best methodology to support children with disabilities in
their growth.

Throughout this study, you have learned many principles about children's behavior. You now know that all behavior is purposeful, and that any behavior reinforced
either positively or negatively will increase. You also know
that for behavior change to occur, parents must change how
they interact with and respond to their children. These
principles are the same for children with disabilities. The
only difference is that the learning might take longer and
parents must be more **intentional** in their training. You will
learn more information about this process a little later in
this section.

First, we would like to share a story of a student with
disabilities who significantly benefitted from positive behav-

ior support. Chris was ten years old when he was placed at a private school for students with significant behavioral and developmental issues. In his previous placement in a public school, he had been physically aggressive toward staff and other students. The public school had called law enforcement to control him when he was as young as eight years old. In addition, his family was frequently called to remove him from school due to his behavior. The school also applied physical restraints as often as once or twice a week due to his aggressive and disruptive behavior.

After placement at the private school, a positive behavior support plan was developed. It was determined that Chris' behavior was communicative. His behavior was designed to meet his needs for attention and to escape activities he had difficulty performing. As you can imagine, his behavior had been successful. He had received lots of attention for his inappropriate behavior at the public school, and he was able to escape activities that he did not want to do by acting out behaviorally and being sent home.

The private school worked hard with Chris to provide him support and opportunities for positive attention. Within six months, he was transitioning throughout his school day without support. Within eighteen months, his difficult behaviors had disappeared, and he successfully transitioned back to a public school. He is now a student at a public high school making excellent progress, and he is also involved in sports and other extracurricular activities without behavioral problems.

## Determine Your Child's Purpose

If you are a parent of a child with special needs, know that this philosophy and practice has the most successful outcomes for children with disabilities. So where do you begin? If after reading this book, you realize that you have often reinforced your child's inappropriate behavior with attention, please do not be discouraged. Begin to think about your child's behavior and what its purpose may be. Use your analytical skills to objectively think about what your child may be trying to communicate. If his communication skills are limited, he may be trying to communicate frustration or discouragement.

Keep in mind that children also frequently use behavior to escape activities that are challenging. If you often observe your child's inappropriate behavior escalate when he is asked to do something that he struggles with, this may be an indication that the request is too difficult for him. Parents of children with disabilities must be patient and accepting of a learning curve that is slower than typical. Putting pressure on your child to learn and grow at the same rate as a typically developing child can cause frustration and greater behavioral problems.

## Encourage Appropriate Behavior with Positive Verbal Reinforcement (PVR)

Once you have an idea of what your child is communicating with his behavior, you can begin to make positive changes. Positive Verbal Reinforcement is almost more important for children with special needs than it is for those who are typically developing. Begin to catch your child doing something right and let him know. Your PVR should be specific, and also more enthusiastic than usual for your child with special needs. Many typically developing children receive such accolades in several settings, but children with disabilities often do not experience this type of support and encouragement in the outside world. Even children with very mild disabilities are often discouraged and feel very unsuccessful. In many environments, including schools and community activities, they may have been targeted for their lack of academic skills or poor social skills. They may be labeled as "lazy," "disruptive," or "a troublemaker," or ostracized for struggling to keep up with academic demands.

Parents of children with disabilities can be the first to recognize their children's gifts and graces. Their home can be a place where they are loved unconditionally and encouraged in their development, which will counteract some of the negative feedback that they may have been experiencing. As a parent, you can help your children see themselves in the light of their accomplishments, rather than comparing themselves to others who may not be facing the same challenges. Remember to focus on their **abilities,** not their disabilities.

## Break Down Skills Into Their Component Parts

It is especially important for parents of children with special needs to focus on clear expectations for every activity that they want to teach their children. Break down tasks to the smallest components and teach each step progressively. What does that look like? Suppose you wanted to teach your child to have good table manners. Break down the steps more concisely than you would for a typically developing child. For instance, you may first teach your child how to use her utensils appropriately. Wait until she is usually successful with that step before going on to the next step of chewing with her mouth closed. And remember to use frequent and enthusiastic PVR at every step to encourage success.

Breaking down skills to their component parts will allow your child to learn each step and to experience success in her achievement. While you may celebrate a typically developing child's ability to tie her shoes, your child with a disability may need to be celebrated for simply putting her feet into her shoes independently.

## Teach Age-Appropriate Expectations

Parents of children with special needs may sometimes fail to set age-appropriate expectations for their children. This may be motivated by sympathy or a parent's need to protect her child. Although understandable, this may lead to "learned helplessness." Sometimes parents can become so concerned about their child's special needs that they do not teach him to dress himself, perform his own hygiene tasks, or socialize with his typical peers. The parents then end up creating a situation where their child believes that he is helpless and must depend on his parents for everything. This leads to greater frustration for the child and the parent.

By having age-appropriate expectations for activities of

daily living and social interactions with typically developing peers, you will provide your child with the skills necessary to navigate in the real world. Remember that children with disabilities can learn. **Every** child can learn. But this does not mean that you should always expect your child's growth to be commensurate with that of typical children. It is important to have appropriate expectations for their learning pace and to tailor your teaching to your child's individual learning modality and preferences.

Determining how your child learns is important to the implementation of appropriate expectations. Some examples that are used with children with disabilities are visual supports for instructions, sensory breaks to relieve stress and improve attention, and frequent reinforcement for work completion. As each child with disabilities is unique, your task is to know "how" your child learns and to utilize that knowledge in your interactions.

## Be Ready to Withstand Pronounced Extinction Bursts

While teaching your child with special needs in clear and measured ways is important, your response to his inappropriate behavior is equally important. Just as you must be more intentional with your clear expectations, you must also be more intentional with your consequences and when ignoring inappropriate behavior. In our experience, children with special needs have more frequently been reinforced both at home and at school for their poor behavior than their typical peers. As a result, their behavior can seem more ingrained and will be harder to extinguish. Your role is to be diligent in not giving attention to poor behavior and being prepared to withstand a more pronounced extinction burst. Because children with special needs may have fewer avenues to get their needs met in many settings, their behavior can, at times, seem more challenging and resistant. Even during these times, remember that your child with special needs desires to please you and to be loved by you. He also desires to please and to be acknowledged by others.

Parents of children with disabilities can be hesitant to discipline due to their child's disability. Again, we emphasize that it is very important to be intentional and consistent with your expectations and your responses to behavior. Clear structure, boundaries, and support—positively provided—are critical components for such children.

## More Alike Than Different

The most important part to remember as a parent of a child with special needs is that they are no different than their typical peers in their need to control their environments, in their desire to learn, grow, have friends, and be loved by others. Everything you have learned in the previous chapters applies to your child with special needs. Although you may need to be more specific and intentional in your practice of positive behavioral support, the steps in this manual are the same.

While following the steps in *Keep It Positive*, we also encourage parents to access outside support that can help your child with special needs in their learning and development. These can include speech therapy, occupational and physical therapy, and social skills training. Understanding the special education system in public schools and other public benefits available can be helpful to your child's future independence and growth.

Many parents of children with special needs have participated in our classes. The children's disabilities vary from Attention Deficit Disorder and learning disabilities to Autism Spectrum Disorders and seizure disorders. The success these parents experienced was eye opening and very rewarding. Parents of children with special needs can feel isolated and overwhelmed with the challenges their children present. As we have stated in previous chapters, it is important to work together with others to help support you in your goal of staying positive with your child. Determination and practice in this method will help you meet the challenges of your child, while fostering a peaceful, loving relationship to last a lifetime.

# PUTTING IT ALL TOGETHER

*Analyze*
*Set Clear Expectations*
*Teach Outside of the Moment*
*Use Strategies*

**Analyzing Behavior** (Chapters 2 & 5)
    Cause
    Purpose
    Hidden Message
    Parent's Behavior

**Set Clear Expectations** (Chapter 3)
    Reasonable & Age Appropriate
    Outside of the Moment
    Clear and Specific
    Positively Taught
    Provide Structure

**Ways to Positively Teach Outside the Moment of Misbehavior** (Chapter 3)
    **PVR** Approximations to Desired Behavior
    Model
    Teach Specific Skills
    Develop Empathy
    Inspire, Discuss

**Use Strategies for Undesired Behaviors** (Chapters 4 & 5)
    PVR
    Ignore
    Natural Consequences
    Predetermined Consequences
    Empathize, Listen
    Short, Singular Expression of Your Feelings

# CHECKLIST FOR ANALYZING SPECIFIC ISSUES

*The 4 W's: What is the...*

**Cause**
**Purpose**
**Hidden Message**
**Parent's Behavior**

**Potential Causes** (Ch. 2)

**Why may my child be acting this way?**
Is he tired, hungry, emotionally stressed? Are there external factors?
May be solved by changing structure, routine, meeting needs, etc.

**Purpose** (Ch. 2)

**What does my child want?**
Understand, teach outside of the moment, use strategies.

**Hidden Messages** (Ch. 5)

**What is my child really wanting or saying?**
Understand, teach outside of the moment, use strategies.

**Parent's Behavior** (Ch. 2)

**What am I doing to encourage this behavior?**
Modify my behavior. Especially insure that I am using positive communication.

# PUTTING IT ALL TOGETHER

- Set General clear expectations with Family Values
- With every element on this page - **always be calm, loving, and as positive as possible.**

## TEACH for SPECIFIC ISSUES

Set Clear Expectations for specific issue **before** the problem occurs.
- Are expectations Reasonable? Age Appropriate?
  - Teach skills when appropriate.

Compliance/
Appropriate Behavior ☺

Non-Compliance/
Inappropriate Behavior ☹

Positive Verbal
Reinforcement
(PVR)

PVR

PVR

## STRATEGIES for SPECIFIC ISSUES (Ch. 4)

- PVR for every approximate behavior = **best**
- Empathize when appropriate (Ch. 5)
- Ignore (be patient)
- Natural Consequences
- Predetermined Consequences (Use sparingly.)
- It is sometimes appropriate to share your feelings at the moment, but do this sparingly. (Ch. 5)

Expect & Withstand the Extinction Burst

## OUTSIDE of the MOMENT
Teach for specific issue:

Encourage with PVRs
- Model and share your thoughts
- Develop empathy, share feelings
- Teach skills
- Share personal stories, feelings
- Inspire, share value of behavior
- Books, discussions

PVR

If there is inappropriate behavior by parent (yelling, calling names, etc.), **apologize** at moment or later when calm.

PVR

# NOTES

[1] Within three years of being released, 67% of former prisoners are rearrested and 52% are re-incarcerated (Langan, 2002).

[2] *Passive-aggressive behavior* refers to passive resistance toward authority. It is a defense mechanism that children often use instead of direct defiance to deal with negative or uncomfortable situations. Procrastination, resentment, stubbornness, sullenness, learned helplessness, and secrecy are examples of passive-aggressive behavior. Passive-aggressive behavior usually occurs on a subconscious level.

[3] DiClemente, 1996, p. 43.

[4] Punitive systems result in increased aggression (with increased tendency toward criminal behavior, aggressiveness toward spouses, punishing own children), withdrawal from punishers and other authorities, withdrawal from positive activities, programs, and institutions, learned helplessness, transference from one negative behavior to another, the imitation of punishing behavior, decreased social status, and negative self-esteem (Sulzer-Azaroff, 1991, pp. 485-490). For an extensive study on spanking and the resulting increase of aggressive behavior, see also Taylor, 2010.

[5] Bijou, S.W. 1988.

[6] Mueller, 1998

[7] Birch, 1998.

# REFERENCES

Allen, K.E., Hart, B.M., Buell, J.S., Harris, F.R., and Wolf, M.M. 1964. Effects of social reinforcement on isolate behavior of nursery school child. *Child Development*, 35, 511-518.

Bernhart, A.J., and Forehand, R. 1975. Effects of labeled and unlabeled praise on lower and middle class children, *Journal of Experimental Child Psychology*, 19, 536-543.

Bijou, S.W. 1988. Behaviorism: History and Educational Applications. *International Encyclopedia of Education.* pp. 444-51.

Birch, Leann L., Fisher, Jennifer O. 1998. Development of Eating Behaviors Among Children and Adolescents. *Pediatrics,* 101, No. 3, pp. 539-549.

Broden, M., Bruce, C., Mitchel, M.A., Carter, V., and Hall, R.V. 1970. Effects of teacher attention on attending behavior of two boys in adjacent desks. *Journal of Applied Behavioral Analysis*, 3, 199-203.

Chapman, Gary, and Campbell, Ross, *The Five Love Languages of Children.* Chicago, Northfield Publishing, 1997.

DiClemente, Ralph J., Hansen, William B., and Ponton, Lynne E. *Handbook of Adolescent Health Risk Behavior*. N.Y., Plenum Press, 1996.

Kennedy, D.A., and Thompson, I., 1967. Use of reinforcement technique with first grade boy. *The Personnel and Guidance Journal* 46, 366-370.

Langan, Patrick A., and David J. Levin. *Recidivism of Prisoners Released in 1994*. Bureau of Justice Statistics, 2002. http://www.ojp.usdoj.gov/bjs/pub/pdf/rpr94.pdf.

Mueller, Claudia M., and Dweck, Carol S., 1998. Praise for Intelligence Can Undermine Children's Motivation and Performance. *Journal of Personality and Social Psychology*. Vol. 75, No. 1, 33-52.

Sulzer-Azaroff, B., and Mayer, G.R., *Behavior Analysis for Lasting Change*. San Francisco, Holt, Rinehart, and Winston, Inc. 1991.

Taylor, Catherine A., Manganello, Jennifer A., Lee, Shawna J., and Rice, Janet C., 2010 Mothers' Spanking of 3-Year-Old Children and Subsequent Risk of Children's Aggressive Behavior, *Pediatrics*. doi:10.1542, 2009-2678.

# A FINAL NOTE FROM THE AUTHORS

## Visual Timer Information

The Visual Timer we recommend is manufactured by Time Timer, LLC, and was available online through websites such as Amazon.com and lakeshorelearning.com at the time of this printing. It has an easily visible red pie piece that decreases in size as time elapses, allowing children to "see" how much time they have left to complete an activity. It has an audible option, but we recommend turning this function off as children tend to become anxious when audible timers go off.

## Additional copies of this book may be ordered through:

Amazon.com, or BarnesandNoble.com or directly through our website at www.keepitpositive.net. For quantities of ten or more for resale, visit outskirtspress.com/buybooks.

## For information on Upcoming Classes, or to Schedule a Class in your area, visit:

www.keepitpositive.net

**For permission to reprint portions of this book, contact:**

juda@keepitpositive.net

Breinigsville, PA USA
13 November 2010
249247BV00001B/2/P